Handbook For A Burning Age

Will Roger

Foreword by

Chip Conley

Essays by

Fred Sigman and Rosa JH Berland

Publication Date: July 2022

ISBN: 979-8-9851003-1-0

I. Will Roger. II. Handbook For A Burning Age III. Philosophy IV. Landscape Photography

First Edition

Cover Photo: Will Roger
Managing Editor: Laura Henkel
Editor: James Austin
Design & Typography: Muhammad Imran
Artist Portrait: Crimson Rose
Principal Photography: Will Roger

Special Thanks:
Chip Conley, Fred Sigman, Rosa JH Berland, James Stanford, Angela M. Brommel, James Austin, Laura Henkel
and Crimson Rose.

Further information can be obtained at: WillRoger.com

To my muse and life partner, Crimson Rose, with whom I love with all my being.

Table of Contents

A desert is a sacred place that is demanding. It compels you to feel in awe of its beauty and harshness.

Forged in Nature: Will Roger, The Common Shaman

Chip Conley

Foreword

"What's valuable in life is what's scarce. And, what's most scarce is ephemerality." This is one of many pearls of wisdom I've learned from my friend and elder Will Roger. It's part of the reason my favorite of Burning Man's *Ten Principles* is "Immediacy." This principle asks that we let serendipity have her way with us and take notice when the magic arrives. Somehow, in Will's company, magic comes with increasing regularity. I first met Will more than a decade ago at a gathering at Fly Ranch.

It was Burning Man 2009, and the founders had their hearts set on bringing the ranch into the Burner family. They erected a stylish, lavish dinner tent for potential donors and community members near the geyser spouting primordial showers. Everyone quickly gravitated to the food and drink, having spent nearly a week or more in the parched Black Rock City desert. Somehow, I sensed the treasure of this sunset gathering wasn't artificial, and my intuitive sense of a hot spring nearby had me turn left when everyone else went right. I walked on a barely traipsed path to an Olympic-sized pool natural hot spring pond with mineral-rich mud ready to be caked on my naked body.

I was all alone in this pond as the sun bid me adieu, and a half-dozen wild horses roamed over to drink from the pond's overflow. At that moment, with the stars commencing their speckle, I was reintroduced to the healing power of Gaia as I felt in harmony with the nurturing essence of nature. Upon nightfall, I realized I was being a bad guest, so I gathered myself up and re-entered the world of humans, at least the Burner version. And, at the dinner party, I met Will and experienced his rapt and reverent appreciation for Fly Ranch. He spoke lyrically of Fly's sensual femininity juxtaposed with Black Rock's rugged masculinity, just a dozen miles away. In that evening, I quietly committed myself to help Will realize his dream of stewarding Fly Ranch as the future of the Burning Man organization.

Decades ago, I learned that a shaman is a "wounded healer," and Will is a perfect specimen. His history – both tortured and tender – has helped him "grow whole" rather than old. Amidst challenging circumstances, he's learned to engage the mystic within himself, and his playground for this magic is often in nature. While he captures images of our sacred land in photos, more than anything, he's helped me to see the fleeting beauty of our bond with Mother Earth. Will has helped me know that we all have a cosmic connection with the wilds, a divine matrimony. It is in those moments that we let go of ourselves and encounter the communal consciousness we have with each other.

Sociologist Emile Durkheim studied religious pilgrimages more than a century ago and coined the term "collective effervescence" to describe the phenomenon of members of a tribe letting their sense of ego separation evaporate while a communal joy emerges simultaneously. In these moments, words have little currency. Our sense of electric current connects us, silent and powerful, and deliciously attaches us, even for just a few seconds that may feel like a lifetime. These kinds of encounters have led to Burning Man being experienced as an epic spiritual gathering, but Will has taught me that this kind of magic doesn't require tens of thousands of people. It can be found by yourself, in connection with nature. You can be your own shaman.

I've spent the past few years studying rites of passage to understand that society has historically created rituals and celebrations to help provide social support for those going through stage-of-life transitions. Puberty: bar/bat mitzvah, quinceanera. Adolescence to Adulthood: a graduation and commencement ceremony. Marriage: wedding. Birth: baby shower. Death: a funeral. But, between baby shower and funeral: NADA! This is part of why Burning Man and transformational festivals have gained such popularity as they serve as a ritualistic modern adult antidote to the tyranny of the dominant culture.

Talking with Will a few years ago, I realized that a new kind of elder was emerging. Not necessarily the elder of the past who was regarded with reverence. No, we appreciate this modern elder for their relevance as they take their timeless wisdom and apply it to modern-day problems. This common shaman is as curious as they are wise. Curiosity opens up possibilities, while knowledge allows one to see what's essential. This process of opening up and distilling down creates progress, and it's a foundation for life-long learning and unlearning. This I have learned from Will.

Soulcraft author and founder of the Animas Valley Institute Bill Plotkin writes, "The vast majority of midlife crises might be better understood as overdue calls to adventure." In this poignant piece of prose, Will, our modern elder, helps us see that midlife isn't a time to conform and submit, but it's a time for rising. When our spirit has outgrown the container of our ego, we become open to new transitions. Like the caterpillar to butterfly saga, we're willing to get liminal, trusting that we will bust out of this cocoon more colorful and ready to fly. Often, our connection to wild nature and deep-seated human nature gives us the soulful ballast to follow the less common path. If you are on the right path, your world should grow much larger in the second half of your life. That's certainly been the case for Will. His books, *Handbook for a Burning*

Age, *Compass of the Ephemeral*, and *In Search of the Common Shaman*, can be your literary roadmaps for this journey.

Your path may require a certain amount of solitude so you can feel the altitude of your soul. Our path to growing whole and integrating who we are is often learning to tell the difference between who we are and how others mirror that or not. Will's journey to becoming an elder was one forged both on the inside – of himself – and the outside – in nature – not necessarily at cocktail parties and festive dinners, which can often seem like a revolving hall of mirrors.

The societal narrative has suggested that aging was all about "growing old," not "growing whole." But, as Will presents in his manifesto, maybe maturing is all about "growing bold." To be bold is to "show an ability to take risks; confident and courageous," to be "daring, intrepid, courageous, brave, valiant, fearless, unafraid, undaunted, dauntless, and valorous." These words describe how I felt after I'd read Will's book. This is the future of the common shaman. This is your future.

Humans are multidimensional travelers. We share a consciousness that is common to us all, the gift of our human evolution.

Preface

Every evening at my home in Gerlach, Nevada, I perform a personal ritual that many have practiced throughout human history. Along with my wife, Crimson Rose, we walk. Ours is not an after-dinner stroll through the neighborhood or one that simply gets us out of the house. The path we follow is circular, taking us through a series of switchbacks and changes of direction. On our property in this remote desert town, we created a labyrinth.

The entrance to the labyrinth faces west. Beyond the enclosure that defines our property, the southern end of the Granite Range slopes downward toward the horizon. It is along this skyline that the sun disappears each day, touching a different point along the ridge as we pass through the year's seasonal changes. We begin our circumambulation timed so that as the last rays of the sun strike our faces, we are standing in the center of the labyrinth. Being at that exact spot at that particular moment births an immediate and direct physical and spiritual experience, a connection with something higher than us that envelops us in its energy.

Crimson had long dreamed of building our labyrinth ever since she walked the one inside of the Grace Cathedral in San Francisco in the mid-1990s. Located near the entry into the nave, facing the altar to the west, the labyrinth in this Episcopal church is a replica of the one found in the 13th-century French

Gothic cathedral of Chartres. Crimson knew that one day we would find the perfect location to make her vision a reality. And so, we did.

One Thanksgiving weekend, Crimson laid out the labyrinth on the south side of our property. She began by placing small black stones to measure the twelve circles that would define the singular path that leads to the center. I added the larger stones. Think of these larger stones as keystones, elements of the Earth that define the circumference and size of this archetypal symbol as a way of celebrating the planet. In many ways, this symbol is a way of celebrating the Earth and seeing humanity as ever-evolving players on its stage. Over time we have placed crystals, shells, bones, and other memorabilia along the path toward the center. Our guests to Gerlach have also made their contributions. We always feel a strong connection with the Earth and the energy of people who have walked with us.

We walk at sunset as the planetary cycling from day to night begins. I'm like all the other humans that have ever lived. As I'm standing and walking, there's a connection with our earliest human ancestors. Since the beginning of our species, we have paused to watch the sunset.

When I go into the labyrinth, I intend to release my expectations and desires. I awaken my five senses and begin to connect with my Three Centers. Walking activates my physical center. My emotional center is engaged as I send out unconditional love to all of humanity. And then the third center, the intellectual, emerges as I open my mind to the ideas generated by walking through the labyrinth. Its shape and primordial concept are reminders of how our minds work.

As I stand in this circle each evening, I know nature is not out there, somewhere other than here. It is right under our feet—the place where we begin our journeys of the body and the soul—the same place where our journeys will come to an end one day. From wherever we stand on the Earth's surface, we can see the extraterrestrial expansion of nature that is the entire multiverse. The awe of the Milky Way, the center of our galaxy, and the solemnity of the rising sun orient our awareness of consciousness. It is not only within the confines of the human mind because true awareness is everywhere and in everything. Remembering that is part of what ritual does for us.

I feel my deepest connection to all of humanity when I walk the labyrinth. As I circumambulate from the outside entry into the center of the labyrinth, sometimes in the heat of summer and often in the frigid cold of the northern Nevada high desert, everything that exists is present alongside me.

From where we stand at the center of the labyrinth, we observe that path of the sun. Our internal clocks become aligned with that celestial event. Sunsets are perhaps the most observed natural phenomena since humanity first looked toward the sky. The solemnity and beauty of that daily ritual inspire our aesthetic impulses toward nature and the Earth as a whole.

As with any sacred place or sacred building, when I am alone in the labyrinth, I often emerge after a period of maybe a half hour or so and wonder where I am. Turning back toward the center, gazing upon the fading color of the sky into the night shortly after the sun has set, sometimes I can't remember if I just completed that short journey. That is the kind of walk when we truly live in silence, open to every word given us from the Earth and the universe.

Over many years, I now understand that the simple act of walking, with the intention of mind, leads us to appreciate the universe in its entirety. Humans are multidimensional travelers. We share a consciousness that is common to us all, the gift of our human evolution. What all humans have in common is a form of heightened awareness, an intuitive understanding of not only the physical world through which we walk but also a spiritual ecosphere. That awareness must be cultivated through practice and being active in something as mundane as walking a labyrinth.

In my last book, *Compass of the Ephemeral*, I shared my aerial photography of Black Rock City, the home of the Burning Man. Photography has always been a spiritual practice for me. The last book was from the sky gazing down on the Earth, while this one takes place on Earth. In this book, I will share more about how my daily photos of my environment are a part of my practice as an artist and a human.

This book portrays creativity as a solution. I believe that artists have a unique ability to use their art for change, but I also think accessing what I call the "creative spirit" is available to us all. Every day can often seem the same, over and over again. This changes when we shift our gaze upon our days until we see them in a new, unique way as each sunset. As a photographer, I have spent my life doing that.

As no one person or book can provide or know everything, I invited my friend, art historian, and photographer, Fred Sigman, to share his insights from his own creative journey as a contributor to this book. His academic and spiritual pursuits are unique, yet are paralleled to my own.

Handbook for a Burning Age focuses on my reflections and beliefs. It is in no way meant to say that these examples and practices are the only way. It's what has worked for me. I hope that you find things that resonate with you, and in turn, share your own examples and practices with others. There's much we can learn from each other. Learning to live more harmoniously with our planet and all of its inhabitants requires not only what we already know, but also what we can discover together as well.

The Road to Gerlach

Fred Sigman

Introduction

ong before scientists discovered the hole in the ozone layer over Antarctica, Will Roger and I embarked upon our separate journeys toward seeking to understand our planet, its wildness, and the sacred and cultural values that have shaped our relationship with nature. In the summer of 2019, we came together in Gerlach, Nevada, to discuss those journeys.

Along the way, Will and I studied various religious and philosophical traditions that helped evolve how we see the Earth. We continue to read writers and thinkers who have expressed the aesthetics of the environment throughout history. Over the years, however, we have done more than sit in our "hermit hut," pondering and philosophizing, and become advocates for change. At times, we are politically active in organizations working to protect our lands, natural resources, and wildlife, such as the Sierra Front for Will and the Audubon Society for me. When I met Will, one of the exciting things for me was the similar paths we had each followed as photographers and educators.

Writing and researching for *Handbook* have led me to re-examine the environmental issues I began to embrace as a 16-year-old in Cohasset, Massachusetts. My stepbrother – John John, eleven years older, and I had a series of conversations when we visited my mother and his father. An extraordinarily well-read and opinionated polymath, he was an inspiration to me. What I always loved about my John John was the fire in his belly. When he saw jet planes on television, he would yell at the screen about how they were polluting the atmosphere. I was already on that same course; he just gave me a nudge in the right direction. John John significantly opened my eyes to what was happening to the planet. That was in 1970, two years after Paul and Anne Ehrlich's *The Population Bomb*, and just two months after celebrating the first Earth Day. This awakening to the environmental crisis, along with my love of wild places, is one reason why I became a professional wildlife photographer.

When I was a junior in high school in Las Vegas, journalist A.D. Hopkins of the Las Vegas Review-Journal accepted an article I wrote for publication in the Sunday supplement of the newspaper with my byline. The article was about global environmental problems. Within a year, I published other articles, one of which featured my wildlife photography from the wetland marshes of Las Vegas. I was invited to speak to the Las Vegas League of Women Voters. The Wilderness Society meetings in Las Vegas, and even a couple of hunting and fishing organizations about the threatened wilds of the Southern Nevada watershed.

Within two months of graduating high school, the Florida Fresh Water Fish and Game Commission hired me to document the reptiles and amphibians of the Everglades region. It was a fantastic opportunity at such a young age to suddenly become a professional wildlife photographer, albeit a temporary one. When they called me for an interview, I showed up with shoulder-length hair and a jean jacket with environmental patches all over it. On the back was a big Ecology flag. I was a hippie on a mission.

During my employment with the State of Florida, I also made a 16mm film on the Loggerhead sea turtle nesting habits for the Commission. This film would later go before Congress as partial evidence for putting the sea turtle on the endangered or threatened species list through the Endangered Species Act established in 1973. Although it took six years after I made the film to accomplish that, it was a moment when I realized that as a photographer, art could make a difference.

Currently, I live in Cambodia, in Siem Reap. It's a town that I've lived in off and on since around 2005. It is best known for its proximity to the largest religious structure on the planet, Angkor Wat. The temple city is a mere six kilometers from my apartment. However, what brought me to this religious landscape is the mystery that fuels my imagination. In the surrounding forests, within the many small village Buddhist temples, and among the ruins of the Angkor kingdom dispersed throughout Cambodia. From this small corner of Southeast Asia, I travel around the continent, writing and teaching online courses in Asian art history and practicing my art as a photographer and a filmmaker. With ideas borrowed from Fritjof Capra's Centre for Ecoliteracy, I often make the art and philosophy presented in my courses relevant to climate change issues.

Travel, a word derived from the French, 'travail,' is just that. It is hard work and can only be effectively pursued if you are willing to take risks. The rewards are that you discover places and meet other like-minded people. On the roads I have traveled around the world, I have visited villages and cities, farms and schools, and stayed in guesthouses and Buddhist monasteries.

I make it a habit to often return to the same places over the years. From the first visit to the second and even a third, the arc of time allows me to see changes in a place and among the people. Increasingly, the changes that I see now from previous visits are not quite so healthy in many ways. I think of Myanmar and how stressed parts of the country have become since they have encouraged more tourism. Tour groups now have a path to their ports of entry. Sadly, places that were once quiet and peaceful are now inundated with busloads of tourists who have a disruptive effect on that fragile environment.

In Bagan, the temples and landscape are trodden upon by camera-wielding, selfie-taking visitors looking for a view. There are so many places where once I could spend the day meandering through the forests listening to the birds, making a few photographs while enjoying the canopy of the rainforest and the surrounding countryside. Now, so many of the trees have been cut down and sold off to the highest bidder.

Carl Jung and G.I. Gurdjieff, philosophers both Will and I had read, spoke of 'synchronicity' (Jung's word) and the seemingly coincidental meetings between like-minded people. There are meanings and perhaps even more significant actions that can come from such encounters. Within a couple of days, Will and I realized that this sort of meeting had occurred between us. Our conversations continued from his home in Gerlach and mine in Sam Reip.

I grew to know him through our conversations and by reading his previous writings about the events of his life, the highs and lows, his relationships, and his love of Mother Nature. I began to understand the meaning of these experiences for him as I listened to his worldview and passion about the planet's current state of crisis. He has a compassionate need to help others to see the problems that have brought about climate change. In response, Will also strives to motivate people to become active in their lives to live more harmoniously with the planet.

Handbook for a Burning Age is about igniting a fire within us all. Like fire, it is also about illuminating the darkness of a world shaped by a dominant culture that has blinded us to life's possibilities and even its purpose. Before we can change or reverse our planet's deteriorating climate, we must first change the climate within our souls.

We wanted to create this wonderful,
transformational place that encourages
a strong connection with the Earth.

Chapter 1

I look at my life in Gerlach now, far away from the cultural crush of the big city. Occasionally, I travel to San Francisco or Reno for business. The idea of being an individual consumer is pervasive in our culture's insidious consumerism. It is everywhere. I'm lucky that I live in the desert. Here I'm not inundated by that divisive marketing that corporations use to cause you to think that I will be a better person if I buy this or that.

In Gerlach, I am surrounded by magic because Crimson and I intentionally made the place that way. For me, I have the labyrinth. I love my gardens. The little power nook in my office strengthens me, and, of course, I spend hours in my art studio. I'm surrounded by objects that remind me of the magic. Crimson has her art studio and her orchid and rose gardens. We share a love for gardening and for growing things. We have now created an aquaponics garden, and the sustainability feels right. There is always something to do at Casa El Rancho because the gardens require tending or other needed repairs due to the high desert climate. It is a place of great creativity for us.

Crimson and I have noticed that our home is transformational for other visitors. They find that they connect to themselves, each other, and nature in an inspiring way. We wanted to create this wonderful, transformative place that encourages a strong connection with the Earth. It allows for nature to be an integral part of our lives. Of course, the labyrinth is very cool. There are also many exciting fruit trees and plants that give us an incredible bounty from the Earth.

We have intentionally created this space that allows for ritual, affirmation, personal growth, and so much more. So, it will continue to evolve as a transformative place by our putting that intention into it. And, when people who visit start creating intention when they come here, it will end up being incredibly inspirational.

The small town of Gerlach is surrounded by high desert wilderness that is on the edge of culture. It is close to where they hold the Burning Man event. Nearby is the Burning Man Project's Fly Ranch, whose mission is to conserve and utilize the property for a more sustainable existence. I am so excited about Fly Ranch for its great potential and the magic it will ultimately generate. When that property is finally open to the public, it will attract many visitors. There's a certain energy to the place that allows you to cultivate with intention.

At sunset and with the emergence of the stars, I find the energy at its peak. As I stand in attention and with intention, looking upward, I realize the joyful potential of synchronizing my desire for Earth's sustainability with other like-minded souls.

Existence itself is such a
mystery to us.

Chapter 2

I am a stargazer. I connect to our planet Earth by looking up into the night's sky. Carl Sagan refers to the stars and galaxies in terms of kilometers and years. I, however, am simply one of the millions and billions who look at the heavens above our heads and marvel at what appears to be an infinity of emptiness. While this nocturnal space may be unknown or even unknowable through physiological perception alone, this vastness with its ever-changing display of constellations, objects, and events has occupied the imagination of everyone who has ever looked to the heavens. Throughout history, human beings are related to one another because of our shared experience of standing beneath the sky in wonderment.

This can be a transcendent experience, which is how we take ourselves out of ourselves to see where we are—a sort of bird's eye view. We can contemplate where and how we fit into the grand scheme of the universe. We ask questions about our existence while standing in awe of all else that exists. Existence itself is such a mystery to us. So often, people will say that looking at the firmament of stars against the night sky leaves them feeling minute and insignificant. I suppose that is partially true. However, we are not insignificant. We do mean something. And that meaning of who we are is intimately tied to where we stand and where we come from.

Once I understood how short a single life is, I thought about all that happened before my time and all that is still to come. I know it seems like a paradox to tell you to live in the moment while also connecting to what was before and what might be, but this is a crucial part of awakening.

When we are awake to our existence, we can appreciate a heightened self-awareness, one that reveals that we are inseparable from the universe. We stand in a cosmic balance between heaven and Earth.

In ancient Chinese cosmology, three realms comprise the universe: Heaven, Earth, and Humanity. The Chinese word for 'heaven' or 'sky' is 'tiàn,' which references perhaps a deity, impersonal nature, or both. Of the three, Heaven is the most important because it is the controlling force over everything. Thus, they named the emperor the "Son of Heaven," granting his authority to rule as long as he maintained a balance of compassion and responsibility. Thus, the emperor held that tripod of reality together. Heaven was variously described throughout Chinese history, sometimes as a natural element inherent in all humans, not just the rulers.

Beginning in the 1970s, as the world was becoming more connected and social and environmental problems were genuinely global, Chinese intellectuals reframed the concepts and philosophy of this triad under the banner of a New Confucianism. They attempted to reconcile ancient philosophical beliefs, many of which had been abolished under Mao, with the present-day world. This meant calling upon their ancestors' beliefs to solve problems due to overpopulation, the depletion of natural resources, and a growing environmental crisis across the planet.

One of these philosophers, Tu Weiming, calls this worldview "anthropocosmic," which positions humans as equally a part of both heaven and nature. In fact, we are integrated into the cosmic order. Given the environmental challenges facing humanity, views such as those of the New Confucianists went beyond mere philosophizing. Rather, these were ideas that help us better understand our place in the world and guide humans toward a new morality that leads us to take responsibility for protecting and caring for all life on the planet.

We have become the de facto emperors of our future, the "children of heaven," if you will. Like the emperors of China, when we fail to uphold our "mandate," every place, every person, the entire planet suffers. As a result, many people today call for a new paradigm, a revolutionary shift in thinking necessary to confront and deal with the environmental crisis that has defined our place in recent years. While a paradigm shift requires an abandonment of the so-called tried-and-true, which did not work, older, even ancient ideas about the world still have relevance.

It is as if we are asleep and unaware of where we are.

Chapter 3

In the early 70s, I was introduced to the teachings of George I. Gurdjieff. The essential question Gurdjieff asked was, "Are We Awake?" I have often asked myself this same question. What drew me to Gurdjieff was his ideas of a spiritual discipline that leads us to a personal transformation. His teachings, and those of his followers, translate beautifully into how we can partially attribute our current environmental crisis to how we are spiritually alienated from the land. It is as if we are asleep and unaware of where we are. Much of the way our dominant culture describes nature and categorizes it as something separate from humans is caused by a breakdown of human self-awareness. Thus, we need to reconsider even the language we use to discuss many of these problems.

The philosophy and writings of Gurdjieff were already quite popular with photographers in New England when I began to investigate his work. At the forefront among those was Minor White. Minor began teaching at the Rochester Institute of Technology (RIT) in 1956 in a program where I would later work and teach, although I never met him. His ideas and photographs have had a reverberating effect on many photographers and artists who understand what he was doing. He taught a series of photographic workshops that were quite unconventional at the time. Minor was inspired through his exploration of philosophical esoterica. He often incorporated ideas and techniques from Zen, the writings of Carlos

Castaneda, improvisational acting, dance, and the teachings of Gurdjieff. Of the latter, Minor's interest was the philosopher's concepts of how we awaken our state of being to become better artists but also better human beings.

This is the key to creating intuitive photographs. Minor taught that to go beyond recording the mere appearance of things, you must be awake to a place's deeper spirit and energy. Minor encouraged his students to "photograph things for what else they are." That requires a way of intuiting what appears right in front of us by using all our senses. This will lead us to even higher awareness.

For Minor, the act of photography was more than taking pictures. It was a profound and reciprocal interaction between the photographer and the subject that resulted in an image that is a once-in-a-lifetime event.

Being awake for Minor required discipline, and it was essential to making meaningful photographs. Similarly, this occurs in the practice of Mindfulness found in various religious and secular traditions, from Sufism to Buddhism and other non-religious meditations. It is how we discover our place.

These creative activities and rather esoteric ideas have fascinated me and shaped much of my thoughts over the years, including my aerial, floral, and sunset photography. How we discover and appreciate our place and home is how this book relates to saving the planet and how we get there from here. It's that simple. Seeing a place for what it is and for what else it might be.

Another concept by Gurdjieff that resonated with me was the one I mentioned in the Prologue about the Three Centers. If you activate and balance your emotional, physical, and intellectual states, you will activate your spirit. When in spirit, there is clarity and a feeling of interconnectedness. This balance often happens when we are in nature or in the act of creating. However, when any or all of our Three Centers are imbalanced, we are not in sync with our spirit. We do not feel a connection to the Earth and each other.

My photography has perhaps been the singular most balancing force in my life. Capturing the beauty of a single rose can awake all of my centers as much as any other activity I pursue. Every day, I rediscover the magic and my intention through my work. I believe that each of us has that capability within ourselves.

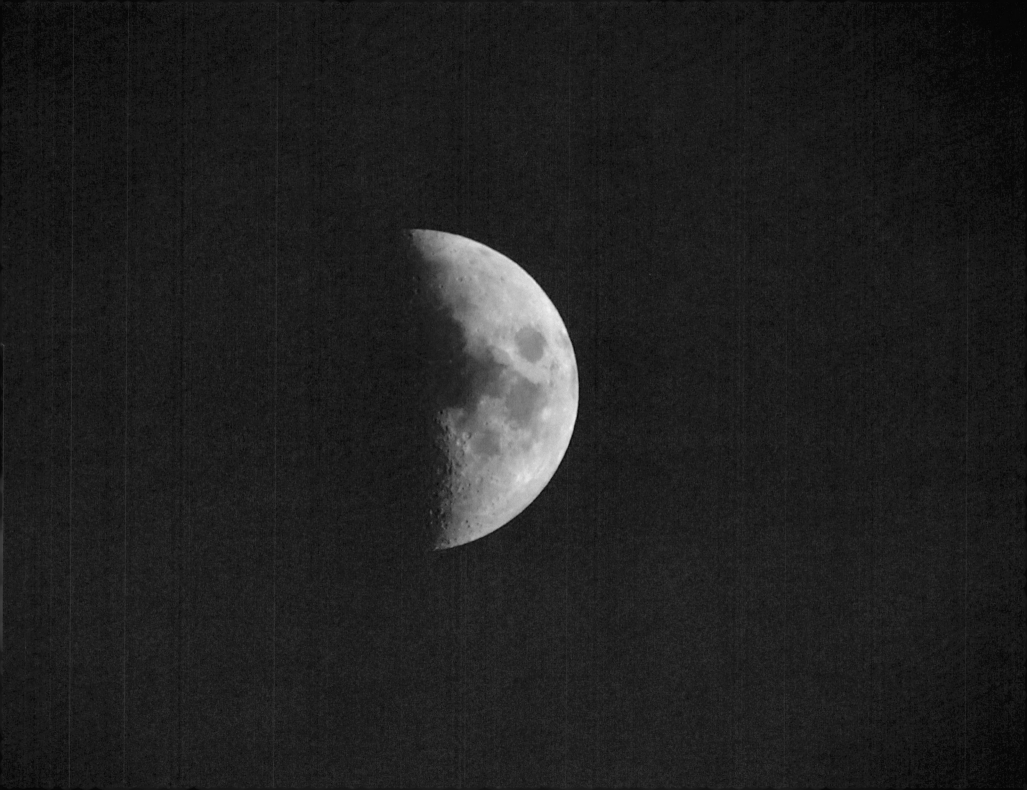

We thought we were going there to study the moon...but most of all, we learned about a new way to look at the Earth.

Chapter 4

A moment of global awakening, if you will, occurred on Christmas Eve of 1968 when the Apollo 8 mission to the moon captured the first color photographs of Earth from outer space. The picture, which brought about a planetwide gasp, was an Earthrise. Humans have long celebrated an extraordinary awareness during the beginning and end of each day. For many cultures, rituals and religious beliefs are shaped around this twice daily celestial event. A sunrise brings renewed hope, while the sunset gives us moments of reflection. This is why Crimson and I walk the labyrinth every day at sunset. It is why millions throughout history have sat on mountaintops, seashores, and on sacred temple grounds from India to Peru to witness the sun touch the horizon.

Many photographs, similar to the Apollo 8 pictures in the 1960s, were taken from unmanned missions to the moon, but the public rarely saw these. On the Apollo manned mission, the Earthrise, as seen from inside the Apollo capsule, was first described by one of the astronauts on board as "very pretty." Bill Anders, the Lunar Module pilot, began to take photographs with a Hasselblad camera and said in a PBS NOVA documentary, "When the Earth came up in Earthrise, I didn't even have a light meter. So, I just started clicking away and changing the f/stops, and fortunately, one of the pictures came out."

He was using a 250mm telephoto lens, which has the effect of enlarging the size of the Earth relative to the surface of the moon over which they were orbiting. In that same PBS documentary commemorating the 50th Anniversary of the Apollo 8 lunar mission, James Lovell, Command Module pilot, further commented, "That picture is probably the picture of the century. We thought we were going there to study the moon. Nah, we went to the moon, we learned a lot about the moon, but most of all, we learned about a new way to look at the Earth." Frank Borman, Commander of the mission, concluded, "The sense of isolation and closeness of our humanity. I wish more people would focus on that."

Environmental photographer Galen Rowell, known for his color photographs made in some of the planet's most remote locations, described the Earthrise picture as "[that] photograph is the most influential environmental photograph ever taken." And it certainly is. Looking at that photograph, knowing that at the time of its exposure, the War in Vietnam was raging on the Earth's surface, and there was global civil and political unrest. Seeing our home, the Earth, as we did, helped put the events of 1968 into some perspective. It was the year when Martin Luther King Jr and Robert F. Kennedy were both assassinated. Hopes were dashed. The world was in political and environmental turmoil. Yet, looking at the Earth, isolated against empty and dark space, it was as though the planet itself was moved by its self-awareness. The picture helped launch entire political and social movements to protect and save the environment, which led to the first Earth Day on April 22, 1970.

Perhaps the National Aeronautics and Space Administration (NASA) program's photograph that gives me the truest sense of our fragility and our precarious existential dependence on the Earth is the photograph of astronaut Bruce McCandless floating alone in space. McCandless was the first human being from Earth to make a spacewalk untethered to the Space Shuttle. This was in 1984 from aboard the Challenger. As he flew some 320 feet away, suspended above the planet, we see his body against the starless black space above the membrane of the Earth's atmosphere. Like so many other astronauts before and after him in low Earth orbit, McCandless said that seeing the Earth from space changes our perceptions of the planet. And it does it in so many ways that you realize whatever troubles human beings are mixing up among themselves, none of that is visible beyond the atmosphere. The problems down below are temporarily transcended. Looking back on ourselves from a vastly different and novel viewpoint makes us wonder.

Why do we behave toward one another and the Earth itself in the way we do?

Why are we systematically and deliberately destroying where we live, knowing that this is our only world?

There are more intuitive ways of thinking and learning that may be our salvation.

Chapter 5

Given the existential threats to continued human existence on this planet, I have to wonder why our dominant culture has anesthetized millions of people to ignore or deny the calamity upon us. There is little reflection and consideration about how we arrived at the place where we are now. Evolution imbued our minds with a creative spirit and imaginative cognition. But we don't seem to be asking critical questions.

All of us are impacted by these changes and activities regardless of where on Earth we call home. Yet, with each scientific journal article, each new study, and reassessment of the ever-changing data, the prospects are not getting any better. Rather, to the contrary.

So, what can we do about it?

I have often wondered when thinking and writing about these issues if maybe it is too late. I am an optimist by nature, but I am also a realist. I came from a science background in Analytical Chemistry studies before becoming an artist and an environmental activist, which took over my life. This is one reason why I believe so strongly in the creative spirit because within each of us, there are more intuitive ways of thinking and learning that may be our salvation.

The clarion call has been sounded before. There have always been advocates on behalf of the Earth, who also were witnesses to the increasing environmental wreckage. These people witnessed the destruction of nature and had to make sense of the consequences.

What is happening to our home, our mother, the Earth?

And what does this mean for humanity, now and in the future?

A sense of wonder toward nature and the universe gives us the ability to look around and see that all is not right. And this is how we will discover the answers to these centuries-old questions.

I am drawn to places where nature is more than an environment; it is an event.

Chapter 6

My awakening to the world of nature occurred in upstate New York, where I spent my formative years in the Village of Kenmore, bordering Buffalo.

This is the birthplace of one of America's most influential philosophical, literary, and aesthetic movements: Transcendentalism. This early 19th-century school of thought was organized around lectures, writings, and organized meetings where the combined interests in Unitarian doctrines, German Romanticism, and even Buddhist and Hindu writings were discussed. Ralph Waldo Emerson and Henry David Thoreau are perhaps the best-known advocates of a way of thinking that says our knowledge of the world comes from the cultivation of an intuitive approach to understanding our purpose through an experience with the wilds of nature. Rational and intellectual reasoning alone, such as practiced in science, was secondary in preference for intense spiritual experiences.

The landscapes of New England, especially in the Hudson River Valley and the Adirondacks of New York, were particularly well-suited as places where the mind of the artist could discover what Emerson named the 'Over-Soul.' That is the universal mind that he defined as "the wise silence" and "the universal beauty to which every part and particle is equally related — the eternal ONE."

A seeker of truth could climb to the top of a ridge and sit on a rock outcropping to gaze out into the valley below and the horizon in the distance. Meditating about where he is sitting and how the world is arranged around and away from him awakens his mind to the interconnectedness of all those particles, which includes the seeker himself.

In the overgrown forests and valleys, a "philosopher's path" could be followed along the ancient trails laid down by early Native Americans, such as the Seneca and the Mohawk. Through these ramblings of nature, a seeker could awaken to the interconnectedness of everything. This is the landscape near where I grew up, and it is the place that brought these philosophers and artists to ask these kinds of questions.

Will deepening our awareness of the mystery of nature and an understanding of, say, the Over-Soul, help us be in harmony with the planet?

We can look at these untouched parcels of land as 'real estate,' with their potential for natural resources, places to clear for human habitation, livestock, and farming. We might choose to build new communities with municipal parks, schools, and hospitals. Or we can leave so much of it alone. Leave it be. As we say at Burning Man, "Leave No Trace." The most valuable natural resource the land has to offer is the undisturbed land itself.

The landscapes of our youth teach us about the importance of wild places. For many people, surrounded by the wilds of the natural world is where they learn a second language. A language that goes beyond words allows them to communicate with the planet and the dynamisms that have shaped it. There are a few places in the world where we can feel nature's power deep inside our very bones.

Wild places may have the sublimity of nature in all its power. The Grand Canyon is one. Uluru in the Red Center of Australia is another. The volcanoes and mountains of Indonesia strike a sense of magnificence that is fearful. For me growing up, it was Niagara Falls, about fifteen miles from my hometown. The Falls are as fascinating for their place in American history as they symbolize the wildness of North America itself.

For me, Niagara Falls and the Niagara River were more visceral than historical but knowing that I followed in the footsteps of a long line of explorers, poets, and advocates is heartening. My parents would take me there for picnics. As a 13-year-old boy, I stood as near as possible to the brink. The deafening sounds of the water were so close, and the thunder of nature trembled beneath my feet. I mean, it was heavy, and with the water plunging over the edge, I could feel my heart being pulled along with it. As the ground shook, I realized that there was a greater power in nature than I ever knew, and I was standing within it. The 'power of place' was instilled in me early in life.

I have traveled to other parts of the world, such as Machu Picchu, but not as many as I would like. The planet is covered with places where nature makes a particular display of its power and why humans have long revered these landscapes. I am drawn to places where nature is more than an environment; it is an event.

Maybe through the relationships you have with other like-minded people, maybe together you can create change.

Chapter 7

started waking up to the world around me while studying Chemistry at RIT. I became empowered because of school. I was no longer asleep. I started reading things about ecology, such as *The Whole Earth Catalog* by Stewart Brand and *Silent Spring* by Rachel Carson, which were incredibly empowering for me. I began to analyze what would be the best path to harmonize with the planet.

How do you make a change?

As one person, I could have gone out and lived in the wilderness by myself, cut-off from culture.

That would have been a solution for my life, but would it have any real impact on the Earth?

I would have lived in harmony in nature. I could be a hunter/gatherer, or I could grow a little food. I would have found a way to survive, and I would have been a different man. My singular life would have negligible impact on culture if I were living in the wilderness all alone.

Yet, alone, how would I be an example to anyone?

No one would be there to see what I was doing! I made a conscious decision that if I were going to change the world and help us live in harmony, I would need to do it by living in the culture. I could not do it living outside of culture because there would be no effect except for one person. Now, if seven billion people all did that, then that would be a great solution. I was not alone in my thinking. Since the beginning of the Industrial Revolution, many great minds already saw that humanity was raping the Earth.

So, how could I make a difference?

First, I knew I needed to work on myself. But I needed to do that in the culture. I needed to be visible so that maybe, by example or maybe through the relationships, you have with other like-minded people, maybe together you could create change. So, I left RIT and my hometown on my journey to self-discovery.

If your inner voice comes up and says, "I am not deserving" or "I am bad," those things manifest. You always want to be careful of what you say with "I am" in front of it.

Chapter 8

I was in my early 20s in the 1960s when I headed to New York City. I was able to find two jobs to support myself. One of them was for an advertising agency in NYC focusing on the war machine in Vietnam. They did not know I was against the war, but they hired me because of my chemistry and wet photography knowledge. My other job was at New York University (NYU), where I ran the Audio-Visual Department. I had access to albums and the listening rooms where students would request to play an album. I would put it on the turntable and then pipe it into the listening booths that we had. I was also able to make tapes. I made reel-to-reel tapes to create soundtracks.

I lived on the lower East Side of New York City, where I was introduced to Theater in the Streets, which had earned a reputation for being confrontational. They asked me to do sound for their street performances. We would set up a portable system that was not easy to do back then, but we did it. Then, they would perform rather activist-oriented theater, usually around Tompkins Square Park. At the time, this park was an important area where political activists would literally bring a soapbox to pontificate their philosophies and radical viewpoints.

The performers that I was involved with introduced me to the Weather Underground Organization and other activists of that time. The Weathermen were the radical offshoot of the Student for Democratic Society

(SDS). They burned draft records and took over buildings. In fact, when I was running the Audio-Visual Department at NYU, the Weathermen came in and took over the building. I lost my job at NYU because of it.

I then decided to go underground for a bit to be with other like-minded people through that group. I was able to get my nerve up to fail my physical and not be drafted. I tried to get out as a conscientious objector, but there was a *snafu* in the documents. I lost that status, yet I made sure I failed both the physical and mental tests. I was coached to fail but succeeded in learning to ignite the activist in me. It was fun to be rebellious.

"Oh, my! This is giving me juice. I feel a sense of purpose, power, energy, and love, too."

I was not confrontational to cause bad; instead, to create good. That was the underlying thing about it—trying to make the world a better place. I was not one of the leaders or at the forefront of the Weather Underground or SDS, but I was a member. I was part of it, and I also had to move away from New York City because of it.

The experiences in New York City opened my mind and further sparked my curiosity about the divine spirit within each of us. I began to study popular divination tools such as the animal cards, runes, the peace cards, and they all began to resonate with me. However, the *I Ching* was most important to me. I devoured the knowledge available to me in each exploration and strived to be the best I could be through practice. I soon discovered that with practice, practice becomes ritual. I also discovered Bertrand Russell's *Ten Points for Intellectual Independence* and his outlook to create a new decalogue intended to supplement secular commandments.

My time in New York City opened my mind to a more expansive way of thinking. It drove me to return to school to finish my undergraduate degree. So, I went back to RIT. I was hired as an employee and was soon running the photochemistry lab. My professors at RIT saw my potential there, and they kept moving me up professionally. I thoroughly enjoyed running the extensive photography facility with studios and dark rooms.

In Rochester, I discovered *The "I Am" Discourses* by Saint Germain. I remember these beautiful books with purple ink that espoused the idea that there's strength in saying the words, "I Am," and this mantra has stuck with me my whole life. If your inner voice comes up and says, "I am not deserving" or "I am bad," those things manifest. You always want to be careful of what you say with "I am" in front of it.

Throughout the brightest and darkest moments of my life, the *I Ching*, Bertrand's insightful 10 points, and my personal *I Am* mantras have given me the philosophical tools to navigate through the unknown and all-knowing seas of my life.

Intuition is like a gift — a mighty gift.

Chapter 9

Upon returning to Rochester, this was the period of my life when I really began to commune with nature. The book, *The High Adventure of Eric Ryback: Canada to Mexico on Foot*, immensely inspired me as it was the account of the first man who walked the Sierra Nevada Crest Trail. Only a handful of people had walked the trail in its entirety. It was the beginning of my quest to learn about camping, equipment, and strategy. Camping became my life, from pitching a tent in my backyard to camping on weeknights to venturing into the White Mountains of New Hampshire to hone my skills.

To trek the Sierra Nevada Crest Trail, you need to be very skilled with your food preparation. It was possible to ship pre-packaged food to fire watchtowers along the trail. Every bit of planning needed to be precise. Food would last if planned right. Preparing packages of dried food weighing 30 pounds each would provide a 21-day supply. My backpack weight would average from 60 pounds without food to 90 pounds with food. Having these packages mailed on specific dates meant there would be no need to leave the trail.

To begin my journey, it was the spring of 1973; I traveled cross country by train. Oh, the beauty of Canada! Just magical. The train traveled near Banff in the Rockies, Vancouver, and then to the Crest Trail above Snoqualmie Pass in Washington. The pass was too deep with snow and impossible to walk. You needed an ice-ax to cut each step. I based my food calculations on 20 miles a day. To do 20 miles a day with a backpack, you are walking from dawn until sunset. Lunch? You pull out whatever dried food or trail mix you can eat while you are walking. I thought I was prepared. It would take time to build up to 20 miles a day. The first day was only five miles. The second day maybe seven. It was a slow build-up, but over the next three months, 20 miles a day was no problem.

Each day I became more in tune with the Earth, the sunrises, and the sunsets. Stars and animals were my guides. The magic started to happen, and my intuition heightened. Intuition is like a gift—a mighty gift. I was experiencing the mystical and living in it. My daily commune with the Earth cycles and nature's rhythms inspired me to discover more. I remember the Cascades part of the Sierra Nevada Crest Trail as being one of the most magical places that I have ever seen.

It took three days of downhill hiking from the Cascades to the Columbia River of the Oregon border. Downhill walking with a heavy load on your back is much harder on your knees than going uphill. At the end of each day, you need to make camp and get your cook-stove out after dark. It was a real struggle at first. Oh, my god. There were a lot of moments where you are going, "What the fuck am I doing this for? Why am I here? Why am I doing this?" And then something magical would happen. An elk would stick its head around the corner of the trail, or I would see a beaver dam with beavers busy at work. The trail took me above the tree line, and it was so stark. There is such an otherworldly look to it. I remember the smells, the tastes, and the touch. All your senses are activated. Back then, I did not have the lexicon I now have to comprehend fully but being in those moments moved me most profoundly.

Oregon was having a drought that year. The scheduled mail packages did not contain water because they assumed that natural springs and rivers would be readily available. This caused me to hitchhike parts of Oregon and Northern California to find food and water. I had reached Yosemite, and then a bear got my food. Another detour! Fortunately, my sister lived close to San Francisco, which allowed me to restock my backpack at REI and resume my hike on the Crest Trail. While hiking the entire ocean coast of Big Sur on the third mountain range and then back on the Crest Trail to Kings Canyon, the high country in the Sierras was incredible. The snow was coming, and it was time to leave the wilderness to the border town – Nogales.

From there, I caught a train to Puerto Escondido to enjoy the warm waters off the coast of Mexico. Puerto Escondido is near Oaxaca. I fell in love with Oaxaca because of Monte Albán and the incredible food. These ruins were awe-inspiring to me. Nobody knows how they assembled those stones. No mortar, no nothing. There were hundreds of massive rocks and boulders. It was the first time I encountered anything created by ancient men. I was left awestruck.

After Mexico, I found my way back to the Marin County wilderness. It was a spot along my journey that powerfully resonated with me. I felt so connected to this area, and I would have stayed there, but RIT contacted me about working there again and completing my studies. My answer was yes. Not only was I made the Assistant Director of Facilities for the Photography Department, but it also provided me with the opportunity to teach photography classes while completing my BFA, MFA, and MS degrees.

Art is a way of seeing and being in the world. It can be a tool for seeing it in a new way, a catalyst for change.

Chapter 10

At RIT, I created the course *In Search of the Mystical Image* for my students to look at gender, archetypes, life and death and how they could personally relate to themselves. In many respects, it was an experiment in consciousness and a way for the students to activate their Three Centers. Gurdjieff was so crucial in the work that I wanted to share the knowledge so that they might engage their own spirits.

My academic pursuits led me to the Caribbean to explore underwater photography. I would spend two weeks a year for five years to dive and create an extensive underwater photography portfolio. For me, underwater photography was the physical center because just doing it was kind of alien – getting underwater and looking at a world that we do not usually see. It was compelling physically to be engulfed by water.

I learned to fly airplanes. I began to fly over these incredible ruins in a plane, and I started to shoot aerials with my partner at the time. We created a beautiful style together. In Peru, I held onto her legs while the airplane cargo door was open so she could capture the most incredible images of Machu Picchu. My art spirit was connected to nature, man's creative spirit, and the harmonious relationship between nature and humanity. I was keen to develop this spirit.

My thesis paper, *Numinous Wildlife*, began to take shape. The thesis was based on the Three Centers, and my photographs could easily be placed into three categories. First, there was the physical center, which was my underwater work from the Caribbean. Second, the emotional part of my thesis was street photography and reflected personal images of my life. Finally, the intellectual part of the thesis was photographing peripheral strip images of time and space. I did this by photographing flowers from my backyard, running film at a certain speed while pasting a slit in the film plane in the camera, using the same speed as an object spinning on a turntable.

American painter Robert Henri and his book, *The Art Spirit*, a collection of "notes, fragments of letters, and talks to students," provided a great deal of insight to me. As a result, I began to develop my philosophy towards art, life, and communing with Nature. Throughout his writings, which I often shared with my students, Henri would weave his art theories and principles of practice and craft into the wholeness of life itself. As he wrote, "There are moments in our lives, there are moments in a day when we seem to see beyond the usual." Art is a way of seeing and being in the world. It can be a tool for seeing it in a new way, a catalyst for change.

For me, art reaches its greatest fulfillment when it represents a culture's ideals that bind the community and link us to the natural world. For this reason, art and nature have also been inseparable. By their nature, they have beckoned the seeker to look within while they seek to understand what lies beyond themselves.

Field Notes: Photographing a Desert Wetland

Fred Sigman

Chapter 11

It was in the wetlands in the southeast part of the Las Vegas valley that I developed an appreciation for the value of the most ordinary and often ignored and abused landscapes. While a high school student, the Las Vegas Wash became my Walden, a place described by Thoreau in words that mirror this riparian landscape, which "does not approach grandeur, nor can it much concern one who has not long frequented it or lived by it." My best friend in high school, Dave, was an outdoorsman who loved to hunt. Our shared interest was in photography and birding, and wildlife observation. Our advocacy for protecting the Las Vegas Wash and the abundance of wildlife coincided with our increasingly radical politics on the environment.

We would head to the Las Vegas Wash with our notebooks, cameras with a wide-angle, and 400mm telephoto lenses in the pre-dawn hours. For over two years, we had mapped every nook and cranny of Wash, giving each of the dozen or so tailing ponds our names. Egret Pond. Open Pond. Hidden Pond. "The Ponds," as Dave and I referred to this area of the desert. This was where the nearby industrial factories sent untreated effluent to settle out before the water seeped into the water table or evaporated. While at times toxic, these ponds remarkably supported hundreds of migratory and resident species of birds. My bird count list by 1972 was a couple of hundred verified species.

The Las Vegas Wash is a kind of wetland marsh in the Las Vegas Valley. The waterway of the wash was naturally formed over thousands of years as rain and runoff dropped in elevation across the valley floor and funneled into the nearby Colorado River. By the 1960s, more people were moving to Las Vegas. The growing population led to the increasing use of local artisanal well water, resulting in higher volumes of treated and untreated water flowing into Lake Mead. Over the years, from when I first photographed this landscape in 1970 until the 1990s, when I returned, the waters through the wash carried significant amounts of toxins, lawn chemicals, street oil, and silt into the lake.

The problems with erosion and general degradation of the surrounding desert environment were further compounded by the increase of flash flooding caused by summer storms that dumped millions of gallons of polluted water across the valley into Wash. As a result, Las Vegas was at risk of possibly losing some of its water allocations from the Colorado River granted in 1922 by the Colorado River Compact. That is the penalty for not managing the unrestricted flow of untreated and highly polluted water into a shared water source.

That is the time when I decided to return to the Las Vegas Wash, twenty-six years after I took my last photograph of a Western Grebe in the tailing ponds. In August of 1998, I drove down Pabco Road off Boulder Highway, searching for that landscape of my youth, the Las Vegas Wash, and "The Ponds." Pabco Road, in those days, headed down toward the "swamps," as nearby residents also called the place.

When I left Las Vegas in 1972 to go to Florida, there were about five thousand acres of cattail marshes along the shores of Wash. By the time of my return, barely any of that landscape remained. Led more by memory than maps, I could not find those wetlands I had once experienced. The words of Aldo Leopold, who cautioned against returning to the landscape of one's youth, echoed in my mind in those first days of return. "It is the part of wisdom never to revisit a wilderness, for more golden the lily, the more certain that someone has gilded it. To return not only spoils a trip but tarnishes a memory." Well, Leopold wasn't far off the mark. The Ponds no longer existed. At least, not the ones where I mapped and photographed.

In her passionate and personal account of the American desert, *The Land of Little Rain*, Mary Hunter Austin described the arid desert environment as a "land of lost rivers, with little in it to love; yet a land once visited must come back to inevitably." Austin's defense of the deserts of the Southwest is her testimony of an aesthetic of harshness. In essence, her observations are those of a naturalist inspired by the heart of a poet. To fully appreciate "the land of little rain," she wrote that one must give the land an entire year, a year in which to witness the procession of weather, light, color, and life. A season to experience all that a place is, all that a place represents. My reading of Austin led me to define a year-long photographic project in the Las Vegas Wash beginning in the summer of 1998. The project is titled *Bottomlands: Photographs of the Las Vegas Wash*.

Since that initial year, I completed two other photographic projects and a short documentary about the once wild and now urbanized Las Vegas Wash. Just as the landscapes I knew and rambled through in the early 1970s had changed or been reshaped, the places I frequented and photographed during these projects of the late 1990s and early 2000s have not remained the same. My camera led me to discover a new landscape, a place, while not as wild as it had once been, retained much of the harshness and relative isolation from the hyperactive urban environment of nearby Las Vegas and Henderson.

It was more by coincidence rather than intent. Still, the first of my photographic surveys of the wetlands near Las Vegas was the same time the Clark County Regional Flood Control District was designing and building several flood control weirs and channels. My favorite spots from years before have disappeared because of large-scale restoration projects, flood control engineering, and the creation of an urban park. Creating a park from what was once a wild and difficult-to-access swamp diminished the wild experiences such a place offered. Such restoration projects, such as the Desert Wetlands Park, weed out the wild, to borrow a phrase from Gary Snyder. I understood why these projects had to be constructed. It was the leadership and makeup of the guiding committees that I often challenged. The building of flood control channels, weirs, and other detentions affected the wetland ecosystems that supported the wildlife. The experience of a wild landscape where a person could explore and discover a unique place within this desert was being replaced with bike trails and interpretive signage along with pavilion-covered picnic areas.

Once I rediscovered some of my old haunts and how the land had changed, I set my countdown clock to 365 days to complete my season in the desert wetlands of Las Vegas. In that year, I might go down to Wash once a week, sometimes every day for a week. According to my journals, about ninety days total. I worked with a Hasselblad medium format camera. As is often my practice, I used only one lens for all of the pictures I made, a medium wide-angle lens. Always on a tripod. My film choice was Kodak Ektar 120 film. I used the slower ISO 25. I developed my film as well. A few years later, when I began to scan and digitally print those pictures, the choice of the film proved exceptional in the quality of the digital images I was able to create. Today, I still use film, some of it the size of a sheet of notebook paper. Damn, I love photography! I wrote this last paragraph for the analog photography nerds.

For many years leading up to this project, I had practiced a method of photographic-seeing that was based less on seeking out the perfect preconceived point of view from where to photograph to one much more intuitive. Paul Caponigro, one of the photographers I wrote about in my doctoral dissertation, has described his pursuit in photography as a "wise silence," a term coined by Ralph Waldo Emerson. Caponigro's small booklet, *The Voice of the Print*, describes how he photographs. "Of all my photographs, the ones that have the most meaning to me are those I was moved to make from a certain vantage point, at a certain moment and no other, and for which I did not draw on my abilities to fabricate a picture, composition-wise or otherwise. You might say I was taken in."

I have always photographed in a similar fashion. Some days I would have my camera and wouldn't take any pictures. One late autumn afternoon, when the overcast light was soft, illuminating the mesquite with tints of green and orange, the shifting changes in color and texture were so subtle, I could not distract myself from that experience by looking through the lens of the camera. There were many moments like this during the days of Wash. It is not necessary to have the camera on all the time. On other days, I was indeed compelled to set up the camera.

When a photographer is still with their ego and opens to whatever guides them to take a photograph, it creates a true collaboration. The meaning of a place finds its way to the photograph's surface through the exposure and development of the negative. That communion is later transmitted to the viewer. It is near impossible to achieve when viewing pictures on a computer monitor, much less a phone. So, for me, the final act of crafting my photography is to, well, make an object we call a photograph.

When we photograph, even with the intent to communicate something to the audience about climate change, or the impact of land development on a place such as the Las Vegas Wash, more will come to us than mere documentation. That is how Newhall also described photographing. We learn about ourselves, and we remember what we have forgotten about our first experiences in the natural world as children. One of the ideas I wrote in my year-long Las Vegas Wash journal was, "…I am coming to understand again the visual roots of my photographic style: why I photograph what I do and why I do it."

My *Bottomlands* photography project ended a year-to-date from when I began. A few days before I had scheduled to complete my photography, a perfect storm of three weather systems collided over the Las Vegas Valley. It produced a one-hundred-year flood event; some even called it a five-hundred-year event. I was down in Wash the morning of that flood, July 8, 1999. I had returned to a site along a channel further down Wash, not far from where the waters flowed into Lake Mead. Beneath a particular cliff, I previously observed a giant beaver, and on this morning, I was able to photograph it, although from afar.

I had planned to return in a couple of days to set up a blind, perhaps. In the distance toward the Spring Mountains, I could see clouds forming over the northwest and to the south of where I was photographing. By midmorning, the tsunami-like waters would soon come pouring down into Wash, where I was rambling around. Fortunately, I had parked on higher ground and was able to get out of there to my truck. The floodwaters devastated many areas of the valley. Several of the flood control projects the county had built were simply washed away. The cliff where the beaver seemed to live was carried downstream. Such was the volume and force of the water. A few days later, I wrote in my journal, "I realized yesterday that every place in the Wash where I have been photographing, all of my 'beaux coins' are now gone. I can never again revisit many of the places where I have photographed this year. The year ended as it began: with an unrecognized and unknown landscape."

Sometime around 2002 or so, a public meeting was held by the Flood Control District, members of the Las Vegas Wash Coordination Committee, and scientific and urban planning communities. The county engineers decided to ramp up its flood control structure construction on a scale that would withstand future events such as the one in 1999. Part of Wash would be developed for the Parks and Recreation Department as The Clark County Wetlands Park. Complete with a visitor center, guided trails, and programming. Out went the wild, and in came the tame. One particular area where I often ended my day photographing in 1998 and 1999, a favorite spot where I would sit in my truck, sip a cold beer, and write up my day's field notes… well, they bulldozed that place and filled it in for the construction of the visitor center. Streaming away from that center into what was once an actual wetland was a series of paved walking trails winding around newly planted vegetation.

The Las Vegas Wash was becoming a manicured landscape bordered by housing developments and golf courses. After establishing a park boundary, developers were free to build right up to the edge of Wash. And why not? It is easy to sell a house when you can tell the prospective buyer, "Soon, all of this swampy and smelly desert will be safe for you to take the kids for picnics and where you can jog and walk your dogs." And there we have it. I did file away 390 medium format negatives from that year—each of them a gem. Two years later, I returned to Wash with a 4x5" view camera to photograph how they transformed the land for public use rather than preserving any wild state.

Every so often, I would discover and photograph a place where construction crews had overtaken the wild. After six months, I made about 225 black and white negatives. Picturesquely grim, I call them. A year later, I started my third project in Las Vegas, which I never completed, titled Dead City, after Mike Davis' book, Dead Cities. These photographs depicted the shifting line of separation between the beauty of the surrounding natural desert and that same land which would soon become real estate for the development as a strip mall or housing development. After that, I think I just got too depressed and didn't go on.

In Las Vegas, we belong to the desert, a place we both deny and accept. Landscape theorist J.B. Jackson described the value of ordinary places and how we should appreciate them as, "This is how we should think of landscapes: not merely how they look, how they conform to an esthetic ideal, but how they satisfy elementary needs: the need for sharing some of those sensory experiences in a familiar place..."

If we are to preserve or maintain places like the Las Vegas Wash, then we must inject into our studies an understanding of some sense of the transcendent and the magic of a place. The sciences of hydrology, ornithology, botany, geology, economics pursuits, and land use must be accompanied by and balanced with a poetic sense of appreciation that goes beyond mere description and restoration. The Las Vegas Wash is more than an environment or an accident in the desert. The Las Vegas Wash is an ecosystem where the residents of the Las Vegas Valley could have asked fundamental questions about why we are here in this desert and what we are doing to this place. We need to stand where others before us have also stood while gazing upon the original landscape. We must go beyond habitat, scenery, and parks.

Wallace Stegner's admonition was that "No place, not even a wild place is a place until it has had that human attention that at its highest reach we call poetry."

As I sit there under the stars, my life often unfolds and reveals the inner child within me. I remember the energy and wonder with the Earth that I felt even as a young boy.

Chapter 12

By 1988, I completed my graduate degrees and moved to the San Francisco Bay area to camp in the wilderness of Point Reyes National Seashore on weekends. Having taught photography for so long, I decided to open my photography studio in Oakland, Provocative Portraits, to provide a unique portrait experience. The concept of the studio was based upon *In Search of the Mystical Image*, which had been developed in Rochester. For my clients and for me as an artist, the experience provided a way to ignite our respective spirits.

By recognizing that creativity, being engaged in our art spirit, and engaging our Three Centers, our minds are stimulated by considering the threads of interconnectedness between humanity and nature. Every thought depends upon a sequence of other thoughts. My photography studio was emotionally, intellectually, and physically fulfilling. I was connecting with my subjects to capture extraordinary moments on film. I spent hours in my darkroom developing photographs. These were the key elements of my work.

My late friend, Rod Garrett, gifted me a garden at my studio. He knew that I had a large garden on my farm property when I lived in Rochester, New York. Rod was a landscape architect and later became the architect who designed Black Rock City. He planted a magnificent Empress Magnolia tree in this garden, nicknamed the "Heaven Scent" magnolia. This setting became my outdoor office where I would sit, meditate and be in wonderment. It allowed me to be in nature while living and working in the big city. Such places allow for serendipity.

In my twenties and thirties, the White Mountains of New England, the Sierra Nevada Crest Trail, and Point Reyes National Seashore instilled an appreciation of communing with nature. My Three Centers were engaged. I could feel the magic around me. And then, one day, Crimson walks in through my studio door. We became inseparable. The chemistry between was amazing.

A year into our relationship, she told me about the Black Rock Desert where Burning Man was held. She invited me to join her, but desert camping never appealed to me. I was rather a snob about the prospect. Where would I hang my hammock? There are no trees, no water, no majestic mountains. She went on her own and came back with all these incredible stories. She convinced me to join her the following year. To say that camping in the desert changed my life is a bit of an understatement.

It is my good fortune to have the largest flat expanse in North America to myself much of the year. On that playa of the Black Rock Desert, there is an emptiness that is the complete opposite of the landscape I grew up around. Yet, like those landscapes of the Hudson River Valley and Niagara Falls, the forces of nature are very powerful in the desert. If the forests of fields of Upstate New York offer the comfort of the picturesque, the American deserts, especially in the Great Basin of Nevada, inspire in us the awe of the sublime. Immersing yourself in this environment is a transformative and transcendent experience.

There is ecstasy and sublimity to such fullness of familiarity. These are moments of grandeur, accessible to every man, woman, and child. You don't have to be a guru or a profoundly faithful member of a church or temple to have a sacred experience. I have seen these grand moments many times at Burning Man where thousands of people are connecting in the same place, liberated, for the time being at least, from daily societal constraints, judgments, political and economic systems, and even certain uses of language. It is about being deeply connected to the natural environment of the Black Rock Desert, where people can create and share in the largesse of artwork and have an open and sharing spirit with everyone they meet while reveling in the pure wildness of the playa. As it was for me on the edge of the roaring Niagara Falls, the connection to a place is redeeming, and at Burning Man, it is magnified and made more potent through the infinite expanse of that desert landscape.

It was a long arc of time that eventually brought me to Burning Man. During those intervening years, my thoughts and imagination vacillated between analyzing the world as a scientist and intuiting and experiencing the world as an artist. My interests in life are blends of the creative power of art and the study of the universe's mysteries through science. I love science and art equally because they both require the intent of looking. Seeing things that have always been right there but for some reason have gone undiscovered. It starts with the simple act of looking. I have always preferred to see the Big Picture rather than all the minutiae of the world. By coming to the Black Rock Desert, I found a way to merge the two.

I have camped in the most spectacular settings. In fact, I camped graciously. I adapted all my skills to desert camping and learned a lot more about it. What I like about the desert is the power of sunrise and sunset. The intensity of these moments is equal to that of the ocean. For me, these are the two places where the power of the sunrise and the sunset can make a man fall in love with the Earth again, feel the mysticism, and feel connected.

Often, when I sit there under the stars, my life unfolds and reveals the inner child in me. I remember the energy and wonder with the Earth that I felt even as a young boy. And beyond that, I become one with the many generations of humans whose intention was akin to mine: the Earth is a wondrous gift to us all and should be cherished and preserved.

As we walk the surface of the Earth, we follow a sacred path throughout our lives from one realm into another.

Chapter 13

My parents always had a garden when I was growing up. My dad enjoyed growing vegetables, and my mom nurtured flowers. While they tilled the soil and tended to their plants, I played in the dirt. I remember crawling around the flower garden bewildered by the colors and shapes. These are some of my first memories. I remember the scents of the soil and flowers and the sounds of my parents preparing the garden for planting. Best of all, I close my eyes and can almost feel those afternoon breezes and the sun's warmth on my face.

I was three years old.

At that early age, I learned how living things grew and the complexity of the relationships and dependencies in what we call nature. I tuned in to the cycles of both the sun and the Earth, especially as we passed through the seasons when the garden activities were synchronized with wherever the Earth was in its orbit. We would put on our dinner table what my father grew in the garden. Likewise, the flowers my mother cultivated and brought into our home were a reminder of the changing beauty of life from birth through growth and finally into death. The idea of raising plants has always been a bit of a magical experience for me. How we can take this hard and dense seed, put it in the dirt, add water, and a few days later, a plant sprouts from the soil, and within three to four months, you have food to eat.

A garden for me means more than pretty flowers and bell peppers. These plots of land are the settings for the realization – an awakening – that we are on this Earth, a rock that has a fragile layer of inhabitable surface and atmosphere within which all life as we know it precariously exists. That is a kind of magic that we are intimately dependent upon the Earth Mother. We do not exist; we cannot exist outside of this protective womb world. Living on this planet, with its diversity of animals and plants, its varied topography from the deepest regions of the oceans to the highest peaks, is like a mandala. As we walk the surface of the Earth, we follow a sacred path throughout our lives from one realm into another.

The memories of my gardens are kept alive as I continue to plant and grow vegetables and flowers where I now live and through my series of floral photographs that capture the life and energy of such beauty.

Up here in Gerlach, along with Crimson, our astronomical observatory, the labyrinth, is surrounded by a series of gardens where we cultivate table grapes, fruit, vegetables and fish, and flowers for their beauty. We often see the title "Gardens of Memory" in association with funeral homes and cemeteries. True enough, gardens do hold memories for the living and the dead. I have always seen the garden as a place where the passage of life plays out on a scale that lets me participate in those processes and arc of time. As a planter and grower, the garden, for me, is more than a place to be admired, as one does when touring the palaces of Europe and the grand plantings and follies of the great estates such as Versailles. Gardens, such as the ones we built in Gerlach, are there to nourish us, provide beauty, and to be touched, smelled, seen, heard, and tasted. When our senses are fully activated, so too are our thoughts of long-ago places and people. We are also awakened to the Earth.

Our gardens were all created by landscape architect Tom Stille, a member of the Sunset Circle. That is the name of a group of 73 friends who I think about each evening at sunset as I walk my labyrinth. The garden adjacent to Crimson's studio is called Four Directions Garden. This miniature park is circular, bisected in two directions along the cardinal axes from north to south and east to west, forming two intersecting paths.

In the middle is a pole with a multicolored wind flag. There are many ancient petroglyphs in Nevada with the same design. Wildflowers and garden flowers have been planted to make natural dyes that Crimson uses in her textiles and fabrics. There are also plum, pear, cherry, and peach trees in each of the quadrants. So much of the beauty of this small patch made from desert soil comes, for me, in the afternoon as the sun begins to descend. The colors, the movements of the flowers, and the direct rays of sunlight passing through are very close to my memories as a child in my parents' garden, looking up through the plants toward the sun.

The other garden on the property is for the cultivation of another kind. Enclosed on three sides, I have built a Zen Garden for meditation. The visitor approaches a gate constructed of four tall poles, similar to a torii gate you would see in Japan. I have made a wall of rough cut ponderosa pine between the outer poles, with a recessed wall to create a dual entry through the middle. The idea is to give the visitor a sense of entering a special place. Inside are three large stones in alignment toward the south, behind which are two chairs against the back fence. Both the gate and the stones reinforce the feeling of passing from one world into another. That is also how a mandala functions, taking the contemplating mind into another realm.

A Japanese tea garden functions likewise as one follows the stone path leading to the tea hut. All these gardens, with their species, divisions, functions, and design, are the small things of the universe that give us more significant meaning to the nature of our existence. We have intended to cultivate our deepest levels of consciousness and create a transformative space that connects with nature. It allows us to be in nature and become a part of it. That is what our gardens help us to do.

The more connected I become with nature, the more I am connected to the Earth energy, and the more creation energy from the Earth, the happier I am, the better I feel.

Chapter 14

C rimson and I have been creating a self-sustaining life here in the high desert. Our first exploration into being sustainable was to construct a building consisting of two rooms. One room is 600 square feet, and the other is 800 square feet. There is a shared main wall with French doors between them. Each room has its own entrance.

Crimson's art studio is on the north side. As a result, she gets the north light which is the perfect artistic light. The main wall of the building that divides the two rooms runs precisely east-west. Gardens surround the building, so she could grow different flowers to be used in dyeing fabric. She is restoring an antique loom so she can weave the textiles that she is creating. Her studio also has big drawing tables so she can do her watercolors and work on other projects.

The south side of the building houses my hybrid aquaponics system, which Gantt Charping designed. The aquaponics garden has a main bed, which is traditional, and a wicking bed where you grow root vegetables in soil. It also has a raft bed to grow herbs, spices, and lettuce. The raft bed does not require soil, but it sits on top of the water that is filled with nutrients from the 400-gallon fish tank. I have Tilapia in the tank, and they are delicious. It is amazing and so good to eat a meal that comes entirely out of that greenhouse. Every aquaponics system is unique. The chemistry of the water, the amount of light you get, the temperature in the room, and more are all customized to your environment.

Some people have their aquaponics system outside and have weather conducive koi ponds or bigger tanks. It doesn't require a lot of money to create an aquaponics garden, and there is a lot of information available on how to adapt it to your specific environment. It is impossible to have an outdoor system in Gerlach because it freezes here in the winter, and it is way too hot in the summer. The big issue with any aquaponics system is to control the room temperature so that the water stays within the range that the fish can tolerate. I lost the first two batches of fish because of the summer heat. Optimizing the room temperature with an HVAC system that uses very little energy keeps the room at 70 degrees. The fish tank water stays at about 72 degrees which keeps fishes and plants happy.

On the property, I have planted 70 trees on a two-acre plot. There are many Juniper trees to break the wind and provide privacy. Along with fruit trees, there is Elm and Incense Cedar on the property. There is a grape orchard with 30 grapevines that produce six different varieties of grapes. Needless to say, we are producing lots of jams and jellies. Concord grape ice cream has been a huge hit. We have experimented with making apple and pear sorbets spiced with nutmeg, ginger, cinnamon, and honey. It has been a joy to plant something, watch it grow, and learn how to preserve the bounty for future use.

So here I am, in my 70s, planting trees and growing stuff. At my age, these kinds of chores make sense to me, and they give me purpose. It is my way of honoring nature at my own pace. Each day brings me closer to understanding my environment better. We are currently investigating ways to use 100% green energy on the property. The idea is to be mindful and respectful. The more connected I become with nature, the more I am connected to the Earth energy, and the more creative energy from the Earth, the happier I am, the better I feel. My dear friend Rod often spoke to me of the power of nature. He, too, was enamored by the magic of the high desert of northern Nevada. I feel it every day as I work and walk in my gardens.

If we can do this here in the desert, you can do it anywhere. The possibilities are endless.

I enjoy working with brilliant people that are working on this project. They all bring a unique talent to the table, and the 'meal' served is truly bountiful.

Chapter 15

We need highly innovative thinkers who can channel their creativity in search of solutions so that we can live harmoniously as part of nature and find solutions that require living intentionally. We need those creative thinkers who will commit to the art of change.

Starting in 1994, I would find my way to Fly Ranch, soak in the hot springs and watch meteor showers all night long. Located next to the Black Rock Desert, it is entirely different from the playa. It is quite alive, with magic reaching out to me. The geyser itself is otherworldly. It has this mystical quality that is awe-inspiring. In 1997, we held Burning Man at Fly Ranch. After we left that year, my co-founders and I knew that the property could be a forward-thinking place to create a real year-round community that lives off the grid. We would create a Burning Man community living in harmony with the Earth, a unique oasis to be self-sustaining and full of creative energy.

Burning Man Project eventually bought the property decades later through the donations of Burners, who also shared this vision. They donated without any strings attached as a gift to the Burning Man community. These gifts were indeed something special. It is common to donate something and expect something in return. One of the *Ten Principles of Burning Man* is gifting with no expectations of return. The acquisition of Fly Ranch was the best example of gifting that I have ever seen. Fly Ranch is becoming the model of how we might live harmoniously with nature without destroying the habitat.

A comprehensive ecological study by Dr. Lisa Beers was conducted for one year to learn as much as we could about the habitat. From there, great thought has been given concerning preservation, conservation, and sustainability. The first program to be initiated on the property is called the Land Art Generator Initiative (LAGI). I highly recommend researching the program. LAGI has initiated worldwide programs that elicit proposals from engineers and artists, scientists and artists on how to make art that makes energy. The only requirement is that it must be green energy.

What is impressive about Fly Ranch is its natural resources: geothermal, sun and wind. It has all three primary energy sources that are considered green. The property is filled with springs, geysers, and aquifers that are carefully protected. With LAGI, ideas are conceived, proposals are created, and activation begins. You can find books for projects designed for Santa Fe, Dubai, and London. The books are inspirational, and fundraising efforts have been successful.

We hope to build some of the submitted proposals. Creating functional, sustainable, and green art will allow Fly Ranch to provide year-round events and educational programming. Sustainability in the high desert is not considered the norm. The high desert is harsh. With creative thinkers, it is possible to elicit an artful paradigm shift for all cultures around the world to cultivate.

One reason I started an aquaponics garden was to show that you could be self-sustaining here in the high desert. And it is possible to replicate it on a much bigger scale at Fly Ranch. My involvement with Fly Ranch is that of senior advisor. I enjoy my role, and I enjoy working with brilliant people that are working on this project. They all bring unique talents to the table, and the "meal" served is truly bountiful.

Preserving a Sylvan World

Fred Sigman

Chapter 16

In the late 1820s, French artists began to leave their studios and exhibition halls of Paris, searching for other places to find inspiration. As they left behind the dread of the city, many artists found their way to the rustic village of Barbizon, about 35 miles southeast of Paris and the adjacent Forest of Fontainebleau. By the late 1840s, the village was a veritable hive of creativity with artists, writers, and poets seeking lodging and their special place – called "bon coin" or "beautiful corner" in French - in the forest to paint within and from nature.

The painter Théodore Rousseau made Barbizon his home in 1836. He would be followed by many more artists, with one of Barbizon's most famous, Jean-François Millet arriving with his family and fellow painter Charles Jacque in 1849. Together, the Barbizon artists would shape a new ethic and morality centered around nature, with the Fontainebleau Forest representing that respect and virtue. No longer did artists need to train for years in an academy drawing from Greek sculpture while studying Homer's writings. While these artists did not abandon all traditions of French art and the academy, they blended their craft toward art that drew its inspiration directly from nature.

For Millet, Jacque, and many other artists, the fundamental reason for their departure from Paris to the forest was Paris's urban and social conditions at the time. In 1832, amidst a time of political turmoil and revolution, Paris was gripped by a cholera epidemic that left 17,000 people dead. In addition, the city had become crowded and polluted with barely any water fit to drink. It was an urban mess. Artists were now leaving the city not only because they rejected an oppressive academic standard of art that they refused to follow but also because their health and lives were at risk. So, they set off to wander among the fields and forest around the village of Barbizon, where most would spend the rest of their days. Long before it became a cliché, these artists understood the return to nature as physically lifesaving and spiritually therapeutic.

When they were not painting, they were advocating for further protection of the forest environment against those who fell giant and ancient oak and who hunted to near depletion the fauna that had long symbolized the spirit of France. The ecology and existence of the forest were at risk of eventual destruction. Fontainebleau might become but a memory in a field of sunflowers. As would much of that part of France, the sylvan world of antiquity was felled for agriculture.

Along the way, the art of nature for nature's sake was elevated and accepted by new audiences while at the same time calling attention to the destruction of natural resources. By the 1850s, a new Parisian middle class visited the forest, or should we say, invaded. They could now make day trips to the area for an afternoon of exploration and to connect with nature. These sojourns were made possible by a growing moneyed middle class and the railroad. In a way, the Barbizon painters may have caused the forest to become famous, thus attracting a new hoard for potential forest disruptors. However, thanks to the artists' political activism, led by Rousseau and Jacque, the forest would finally be protected by a decree signed by Napoléon III in 1853. The basis of setting aside much of the forest was to prevent further logging and exploitation. Overcrowding in some areas of the forest due to tourism and Parisian day trippers was also becoming a problem. In 1861, the government added more sections of land for the protection of the woods.

This forest is relatively small compared to American national parks. And for some, the story of the Barbizon artists, later joined by photographers such as Gustave LeGrey, may seem quaint. But their movement to save this forest, a woodland which had long been viewed as a symbol of French character and history, was a battle. The politics at the time and complications of land ownership made their task exceedingly difficult to preserve this forest. Eventually, a plaque was installed near the village that announced the formation of this new national park in 1851, which was also designated as a "Refuge for Artists." Imagine that.

> *"Nature yields herself to those who trouble to explore her, but she demands an exclusive love... Art is not a picnic; it is a struggle, a grinding mill." - Jean-François Millet*

> *"...the beautiful is in nature and is found in the most diverse forms in reality. As soon as it is discovered there, it belongs to art, or rather to the artist who knows how to see it. As soon as the beautiful is made real and visible, it has its artistic expression in itself. But the artist has no right to amplify this expression. He can touch it only at the risk of changing its nature and consequently weakening it. The beautiful given by nature is superior to all the conventions of the artist." - Jules Antoine Castagnary*

Today there is much scientific inquiry into how trees communicate. While at first laughable, then controversial, and now growing in acceptance, scientists are beginning to think in terms that indeed trees do talk to one another. In his book, *The Hidden Life of Trees: What They Feel, How They Communicate*, German author and forester Peter Wohlleben identifies the form of speech as occurring through a series of "underground fungal networks. Trees share water and nutrients through the networks and also use them to communicate.

They send distress signals about drought and disease, for example, insect attacks, and other trees alter their behavior when they receive these messages." Other scientists have begun to hear the trees speak, as it were.

Thèodore Rousseau intimately knew this over a century ago because of his years of rambling through the forest. Of all the Barbizon painters, his paintings of the trees are the best known. Sure, if you are an artist in a forest, you couldn't help but paint trees. But his trees, well, those paintings also have a spiritual resonance to them. It is as if each tree is sitting in his studio for its portrait. He illuminates the trees with a wondrous glow adding character to the trunk, roots, or crown of branches and leaves. In many of his forest landscapes, he paints a revelatory opening through the trees, revealing a world beyond the mysterious silence of the forest. There is a clear distinction between the inner and outer worlds of nature and even our human beingness. When speaking to his friend and patron Alfred Sensier in the 1850s, Rousseau described his experience with trees that foresaw what scientists are now seeing:

> *"The tree which rustles and the heather which grows are for me the grand history, that which will not change. If I speak well their language, I shall have spoken well the language of all times.*
>
> *I heard the voices of the trees, the surprises of their movements. Their varieties of form and even their peculiarity of attraction toward the light had suddenly revealed to me the language of the forest. All that world of flora lived as mutes, whose signs I divined, whose passions I discovered. I wished to converse with them and to be able to say to myself, through that other language, painting, that I had put my finger upon the secret of their grandeur."*

The environmental movements of the 1960s and '70s led many artists to address issues involving nature: how we look at it, how we preserve it, how we destroy it. Artists were questioning the role art could play in protecting the environment. Among these artists have been numerous photographers who take their cameras back into scenes of the picturesque and sublime, places we have customarily seen through the lenses of photographers such as Ansel Adams. The new generation of artist-photographers attempts to show that nature is more than a grand spectacle, a black and white world of glorious light and scenery. There is a dark side to the light; a world abused and polluted, places often hidden from view and ignored by the scenery-seeking photographers who see nature as a calendar or a "Kodak moment." Using the power of the published book, with its ability to reach an audience larger than an art gallery, many of these photographers have used their art to call attention to the issues facing the fragile environments of the American West. The book *A Doubtful River* (2003), with photographs by Peter Goin and Robert Dawson, examines how the Truckee River in northern Nevada has long been dipped into various human uses, leading to increased pollution of an important water source in this arid land.

Since 1979, photographer Richard Misrach has been photographing the deserts of the American West in a continuing series titled *Desert Cantos*. A canto is a literary device that serves as a subdivision in epic poetry. For Misrach, there is the overarching epic of the West, with each canto representing a particular environment, locale, or event upon the land. The landscapes which make up Misrach's cantos are photographed with an 8x10" view camera from which he makes large-format color photographs. The view camera is of a considerable size requiring a series of mechanical adjustments and exposure calculations that determine the lens settings. Photographing with a view camera allows for a slow contemplation of what lay before the lens. In fact, given the time it takes and a bit of labor to set up, the photographer has already recognized the character or spirit of the place that captured his gaze for a few moments before setting up to photograph it. While the camera requires a refined technique of reckoning, conceiving the composition comes intuitively through the interaction with the land. As Misrach explained in a 2006 interview in the New York Times, *Beauty as a Firebomb in the War on Nature* by Philip Gefter, "When the light is great, I go crazy inside. If I go out there with a specific idea in mind, it never works out."

Part of the craft of being a photographer is the ability to combine the techniques needed to take a picture into a seamless experience and to allow the creative energy to bear on the moment when pressing the cable release. Misrach has explained that to make beautiful photographs of the sublimity of the American deserts, you cannot ignore the intrusions of humans into that landscape.

Beaumont Newhall (1908 – 1993) was one of the medium's preeminent historians and writers about both the history of photography and its contemporary practitioners. He was instrumental in founding the Photography Department at the Museum of Modern Art in New York in 1937. His support and exhibitions of many photographers contributed to their careers, such as Ansel Adams and Edward Weston. For Newhall, the defining quality of photography that establishes it as a form of artistic expression is the photograph as a document. He felt that no other two-dimensional visual medium, such as painting or printmaking, share this power on par with photography. In his essay, *Documentary Approach to Photography*, published in 1938, he states:

> *"The documentary photographer is not a mere technician. Nor is he an artist for art's sake. His results are often brilliant technically and highly artistic, but primarily they are pictorial reports. First and foremost, he is a visualizer. He puts into pictures what he knows about, and what he thinks of, the subject before his camera. Before going on an assignment, he carefully studies the situation which he is to visualize.*

He reads history and related subjects. He examines existing pictorial material for its negative and positive value to determine what must be revisualized in terms of his approach to the assignment and what has not been visualized.

But he will not photograph dispassionately, but he will not simply illustrate his library notes. He will put into the most effective way to teach the public he is addressing. After all, is not this the root meaning of the word 'document' ('docere,' 'to teach')? For this reason, his pictures will have a different and more vital quality than those of a mere technician. They will even be better than those of a cameraman working under the direction of a sociologist because he understands his medium thoroughly and is able to take advantage of its potentialities while respecting its limitations. Furthermore, he is able to react to a given situation with amazing spontaneity."

As a means of artistic expression and journalistic documentation, these are the photographic processes we are advocating for as part of our climate change activism. We should strive for a well-crafted and thoughtful photograph. Artists should consider the aesthetic quality of their pictures, when appropriate, as a capable vehicle for communicating their message.

Photographers have used ideals of beauty and aesthetic principles for their powers of persuasion and impact to bring to the audience an increased awareness and appreciation of the world. This approach has been used when the photograph's subject threatens environmental degradation and attacks on nature. One example is the photographer John Pfahl and his series titled *Power Places* (1980 through 1984). In this body of work, we are shown places in America with power generating plants such as coal, nuclear, and solar. The power generating plant is often minuscule in scale within the overall landscape, with more attention given to the surrounding scenery. The beauty of the landscape may lull the viewer into accepting a balance of nature between the industries of power. Pfahl is well aware of the pictorial methods he uses when making these photographs aestheticize and idealize a view of nature. He writes on his website, "It is not without trepidation that I have appropriated the codes of 'the Sublime' and 'the Picturesque' in my work. After all, serious photographers have spent most of this century trying to expunge such extravagances from their art."

That is the ironic twist of "power places." The phrase refers to a place in nature where a person can draw upon the natural and creative energies of the Earth. Unlike the nuclear generator or the coal-burning power plant, those power places are regenerative, not destructive, or potentially dangerous. A power place, in this sense, is a sacred landscape.

> "One of the curses of art is 'Art.' This filling up of things with 'decoration,' with by-play, to make them 'beautiful.'" - Robert Henri, The Art Spirit

Environmental photographers throughout the world are now pointing their cameras away from the magnificent and the scenic. Instead, they now focus on the reality of how humans are dramatically and destructively changing the planet's surface, poisoning the depths of the oceans, and destabilizing the atmosphere enveloping all of us together. Many climate change triggers are visible for all to see through many industries, waterways, mining tailing ponds, and military bombing ranges.

Canadian photographer Edward Burtynsky creates large-format color photographs of mines in Australia, shipbreaking yards in India and Bangladesh, manufacturing and urban environments in China, and home steading in Canada. His website states, "From the beginning of his career, Burtynsky was attuned to the delicate balance that exists between humans and the environment." In this case, the use of the word environment best describes his photographs and the work of the photographers we are discussing. Environment, as in environs, refers to what is local rather than what is global. His photographs depict another reality of climate change by directing our attention to many of its causes that we can observe in our backyards, and not all of which have to do with carbon emissions into the atmosphere.

An Art of Our Own

In the early years of the twentieth century, Romanian sculptor Constantin Brancusi recognized the history of art from around the globe, Africa, China, the ancient Greeks, and medieval Europe. The art of those places and periods embodied their collective joys and aspirations. As Europe entered a new century, he said, "It is time we had an art of our own." That century would undoubtedly go through more changes, revisions, adaptations, and morphing than any generation of an artist before. New technologies gave way to new ways of seeing, new forms of craft, and new ways to make and experience works of art. During the twentieth century, modern artists also responded to events and circumstances they had never faced either. World War I gave rise to Italian Futurism, Dada, and Surrealism. The later movement published their *Manifesto of Surrealism* in 1924, written by André Breton. Like art and political movements, Surrealism was also a social force attempting to subvert language, believing a new form of communication was needed to express post-War Europe. It was especially true since the old forms of expression and communication were also responsible for the deceptions that led to the war.

Throughout the 20th century, artists continued to craft and invent ways of seeing to reflect the times they lived. As the past became increasingly irrelevant, artists formed collectives and movements that advocated social change or promoted a spiritual belief, all in the service of forging a new future based upon notions of progress. While the Italian Futurists celebrated industry and the new machine age, German Expressionists believed society was due for a renewed spiritual awareness. Words such as 'dynamism' and 'metaphysical' were expressive of new styles and models of aesthetics in art, particularly painting. Artists were no longer bound by academic restraints and the past narratives, a history stretching back to the Renaissance. Artists saw themselves as visionaries who looked toward a hopeful future. The social power of art was in calling attention to local and global questions and affairs to affect change.

Today, artists continue to bring their visual conversation ideas from anthropology to geology. Existentialism and shamanism. Farming and digital technology. The driving force for many artists working on environmental and climate change issues is to seek and create opportunities to present their art through public works projects such as installations and performances. Many artists a generation ago aimed to find gallery representation that would lead to museum exhibitions that would establish a career path through patronage and collecting. Now, artists seek collaborations with teams.

The Cult of Genius is irrelevant in a world where we need like-minded creative people working in a community rather than merely an ego-driven form of creating art.

We need to ask questions about the power of art to affect these changes.

Can artists help save the planet by averting human-caused climate change through their work?

Do works of art rise to the status of being taken seriously enough by leaders, politicians, fossil fuel CEOs that they will have their minds changed by what they see in film, photography, sculpture, music, and poetry?

Will the messages of climate change in the Off-Broadway musical, *Hooked on Happiness*, or the play *Continuity* (both from 2019) reverberate through the halls of Congress (as the play *Hamilton* did) enough to sway votes in favor of climate change initiatives?

Artists and documentarians produce works intended to awaken people to what is going on around the planet. They realize it is the collective voice of other image-makers that has a rolling effect on people's awareness. But "Save the World" through art? Or are we just preaching to the choir?

Just as we find a sameness to the highly saturated pictures of wilderness and nature, we have perhaps become numb to the images of impoverished children in the Andes. After a time, these pictures may not move us to send our twenty dollars a month. Not that the problems of global poverty and inequity have been eradicated. We know that is not so. But the advertising campaigns do not have much of an effect on us. Call it poverty fatigue.

Will this happen, or is it already happening, that pictures of environmental pollution and the impact of climate change will produce a similar form of weariness?

Art critic Suzi Gablik in her essay, *The Ecological Imperative: Making Art as if the World Mattered*, writes,

> *"Time is running out with respect to many of these environmental threats, and as we in the late-twentieth-century witness the frightening portents of the beginning of the end of industrial civilization, we are still groping for the answers to many difficult questions about what life after industrialism will be like and how we will adapt to it. As an art critic in the 1990s, I am no longer interested in writing art reviews or catalog essays. Rather, I am concerned with understanding our cultural*

myths and how they evolved; how artists are now addressing the changes that must be implemented in our consciousness and our society."

Many unbelievers in climate change, or the anthropogenic cause of climate change, scoff whenever we discuss the Earth, nature, and our moral and spiritual connection to the planet. But a well-informed artist, whose intention is to make art about these issues, can help overcome these perceptions from some of the public. Such as when we speak of beauty and craft, we want to be clear that while these are some of the skills needed for art to be successful, it is not for that sake alone we make art. We are advocating for creating art that is committed to these concerns of meaning and value.

In a world where most people see works of art not in a museum or gallery but through corporate media channels and social media platforms, artists have a real challenge. They must not only produce works of art that are thought-provoking and emotionally moving, but they must make them available in contexts away from the computer screen but not necessarily through the institutions of commercial art galleries. The human soul needs stimulation to imagine possibilities of change. It requires a redefined method of delivery and presentation.

We need artists working within their ecologies of ideas and shared principles. Artists who believe in the craft and aesthetics of the objects they make also realize the importance of a moral imperative to create art that ultimately is not about them. Community expression rather than self-expression. Or art that gives an expressive channel for the Earth itself, much like the ancient Taoist and Ch'an (Zen) painters of ancient China.

Instead of the romantic image of the solitary artist struggling against the world, suffering in the cold of a Parisian garret for his art, we need educated, proficient artists in their craft and community organizers.

Historians. Entrepreneurs. Public speakers. Philosophers. People who understand natural systems. They are Eco-Aware.

For many people in America, art is mostly irrelevant. Art is usually seen as only satisfying those who seek a world of beauty and comfort, one far removed from a world of turmoil. Art is for an escape, a kind of refuge from the problems of the world. In this sense, art is akin to how people choose to experience nature, also a place of retreat. Art should uplift and inspire, yes, but to action, not complacency. It has been forty years (as of this writing) since the assassination of musician John Lennon. Thanks to him, people of my generation are ever mindful of the *broader social benefits of art,* as Lennon expressed in his music. Even when art resonates deeply within each of us and for different reasons, it also binds people together to consider a higher cause or purpose.

To restore the world and save the planet, we need to reactivate the wilderness spirit already within us.

Chapter 17

Larry Harvey would use the word 'magic' to define the charged atmosphere of spirit, love, and honesty that we were all surrounded by at Burning Man. He often appealed to people to "see the magic that is everywhere around." "Seeing" the wholly other might also leave one temporarily without words, silenced, wondering, "what was that?" It is mysterious. Like I had written many years ago, this was numinous wildlife.

This is the kind of emotional and spiritual arousal discussed among the Transcendentalists when they were in the wilds of New England. A 'mysterium tremendum,' or a mystery so profound as to overwhelm our feelings. The mysterious or unknowable has long moved us to a place of silence and solitude. In a way, this paragraph could also be read as a characterization of much American art.

We have indeed built a world that has made us forget that we are part of nature. And that manufactured world has been the very mechanism that has produced the global crisis now at hand. To restore the world and save the planet, we need to reactivate the wilderness spirit already within us. We need to take ourselves back to that center of the numinous.

A desert is a sacred place that is demanding. It compels you to feel in awe of its beauty and harshness, yet it somehow equalizes its indifference to you. You come and go, hopefully leaving no trace, and still survive. Indeed, the power of that place is what I think makes our annual Burning Man event so successful. Closer to nature, the stars are beautiful, and there is an extremeness of weather. In creating and participating in this landscape, you become an artist. And as every artist knows, there is magic when you enter that kind of place. There is also a sense of faith and belief—the core seeds of the creative process.

Standing in the middle of the Black Rock Desert is to feel as though you are in the center of the universe. I survey the immensity of the desert landscape laid out before me in all its majesty. This massive playa embraces me with its serene energy. As my gaze continues upward, especially at night, celestial bodies appear to orbit and surround me. I am indeed at the focal point, feeling as though at the center of the Milky Way itself.

From that position, you can see everything around you. Even though you are in plain sight, you cannot be seen from a distance. You are at once visible and invisible. The grandeur of this Earthly community makes me both a tiny creature and a leading player on its stage. That is the sensation that excites me to my bones, channeling a dynamic force that runs through me from all directions. It may seem cliché to say, but yeah, I do feel as though I am one with the universe during those rare moments alone.

Let's take it a step further, in the context of not standing in a vast desert expanse. Not everyone is here. Not everyone can be here. Yet, we must recognize that no matter where we are, we are a part of nature. Nature is wherever you stand. In the heart of a bustling metropolis, passengers are in the midst of nature as they are equally a part of nature on that subway. What they breathe in and exhale are elements of nature. Given everything we can grasp through our senses and determine with our intellect and spirit, we should be aware that nature is inescapable. Our responsibility is to find ways to commune with nature, live harmoniously with nature, be creative, and activate our Three Centers to feel the magic and empower others to make our environment, our world inspirational.

The elixir to a great life is mindfulness, collaborating with creative thinkers, providing ourselves the opportunity to connect us to the Earth, sustainable living, and cultivating the spirit within.

Chapter 18

Looking back at my life and the journey, it was inevitable that I would become a social, cultural, and environmental activist. By searching for truth, my activism has led me here. There is a lovely written essay by William Fox, Executive Director for Center for Art + Environment, in my book, *Compass of the Ephemeral*, which discusses the beauty of the Black Rock Desert. In that essay, he describes the desert's uniqueness, history, and the value of preserving the land.

Stewarding Burning Man's Desert Operations for and creating the Department of Public Works, the unit responsible for building Black Rock City and then leaving no trace, required me to share experiential knowledge while working cohesively with the Bureau of Land Management (BLM). I then took a role within the organization to serve as legal advisor to the general counsel to help facilitate the complex nuances of local, state, and federal governments. Being involved in Nevada politics was inevitable. Becoming so familiar over time with all operational facets to produce the event, understanding the environment of where the event was held, and developing sound community relationships in Northern Nevada; it was a great honor to serve as the Chairman of the Burning Man Project for seven years.

I was invited to serve as a Sierra Front Northwestern Great Basin Resource Advisory Council member to provide my expertise on dispersed camping. This council was a division of The Resource Advisory Council

(RAC), a citizen's advisory group mandated by Congress to provide insight, information, and expertise to help the BLM manage public lands. Members of the council consisted of an archaeologist, a botanist, a geologist, representatives of Native American tribes, public servants, and corporate interests. If you visit the RAC website, it shares information to understand various land issues better. Serving on this council and later becoming chair, I was able to see parts of the wilderness that are much more remote than I had ever seen. Having the opportunity to develop relationships with the Summit Lake and Pyramid Lake tribes has been one of the most rewarding experiences. One of the proudest moments of serving as Chair was to support the Summit Lake tribe to divert the Ruby Pipeline around one of their sacred burial grounds.

Friends of the Black Rock was also created to take care of the land of the Black Rock Desert and work with the BLM and with Fly Ranch. Being involved in this organization has also been a sense of pride for me. Of course, it would be nice to see less national and more local governance of public lands. I do not think that someone looking at a computer sitting in Washington has the proper knowledge to make decisions that affect people living in unfamiliar areas. Our Congressional representatives in Washington do not have the insight, information, or interest to help people in local communities fully. It is essential to encourage local governments to assume the responsibilities of the federal government in this regard.

I have had a fascinating life and feel remarkably connected to the world around me. Of course, I wish I were younger, but that is what everyone my age wishes. Even in your 70s, there is humor in accepting who you are. I look forward to the next part of my life. I will continue participating in Burning Man, lecture at environmental and urban planning conferences, tend to my garden, walk my labyrinth with Crimson and take photographs.

Fly Ranch is Burning Man's 3,800-acre ranch in Northern Nevada. The land is home to Fly Geyser, hot springs, three reservoirs, wetlands, animals, and more than 100 types of plants.

Crimson had the idea and wrote a proposal to build a traditional Chartres Labyrinth at Fly Ranch in 2019. We started in May, and we worked on it about 2-3 days a week for 3-4 hours a day. It is a 12 circuit labyrinth that is 104 feet in diameter, with 4 foot wide pathways for accessibility. We finished the stonework in November. We will continue to embellish the stonework this winter, weather permitting, but the basic form is done. We will see how the grazing animals negotiate it on the Hualapai Flat.

So now there are two labyrinths to walk, and I welcome you to partake. The elixir to a great life is mindfulness, collaborating with creative thinkers, providing ourselves with the opportunity to connect us to the Earth, sustainable living, and cultivating the spirit within. This vision has and always will be my calling. It was important for me to scribe *Manifesto for a Burning Age*. For me, this is how we get there from here.

Desert Songs: The Art of Will Roger

Rosa JH Berland

Afterword

"The desert could not be claimed or owned—it was a piece of cloth carried by winds, never held down by stones, and given a hundred shifting names... Its caravans, those strange rambling feasts and cultures, left nothing behind, not an ember. All of us, even those with European homes and children in the distance, wished to remove the clothing of our countries. It was a place of faith. We disappeared into landscape."

- Michael Ondaatje, *The English Patient*

Artist, Author, Teacher, Innovator and Environmentalist

The desert of North America and beyond is a place of enduring mystery, power, and natural beauty. But, unfortunately, many have a misconception that this space of Earth is a blank canvas. Generations have so often believed that the desert could be owned, harnessed, conquered, and taken. The winds of time show such ambitiousness the truth through veils of heavy sand – blinding, erasing, wounding, starving, and burying man's ill-founded ambitions. Yet, for all its unrelenting power, beauty, and majestic spirit, many artists have come to love, respect, and even fear the desert. This dualistic way of interacting with nature is very much at the core of American artist Will Roger's photographic practice and, indeed, his intention in life.

Will is a conservationist, creator, and teacher. He has served as Chairman of Sierra Front, Northwestern Great Basin Resource Advisory Council, and President of the Friends of the Black Rock-High Rock. Will is the sort of forward-looking artist and radical thinker you would want to know and should. We could all learn from his unbridled openness and fearlessness of his intention with humanity.

So, after encountering his work, it is no surprise that this man is also a cultural co-founder of Burning Man, a network of people who share a collective spirit to pursue a more creative and connected existence with the Earth. Will discovered Burning Man in 1994 through his life partner Crimson Rose. Together with several others, they co-founded Black Rock City, LLC, which has overseen the Burning Man event for nearly twenty years. In his work, Will entreats his audience to open themselves to the power and mystery of the natural world. This could be from a panoramic aerial perspective of the Black Rock Desert, the multifaceted and intellectually engaging black-and-white photography, or his deeply sensual studies of flowers. There is a playful fluctuation between object, participant, viewer, and voyeur.

Will began in analytical chemistry, working as a photo chemist at the Rochester Institute of Technology. Interested in finding new ways to understand the world, he went on to earn his MFA in photography and serve as an Associate Professor of Photography at RIT, working at the prestigious institute for twenty years. There, he created and taught the course *In Search of the Mystical Image.* Today, Will is known for his creative formal or technical approach, notably a distinctive style of stop-motion photography. Many respect his work for its fluency of movement, certain enigmatic lyricism, and a genuinely esoteric quality that fascinates and inspires.

As one develops intellectually and artistically, physical movement is often the impetus for real growth. So, seeking a new space and challenge, in the early 1990s, Will decided to move to California and focus on portraiture. He would eventually become involved in the gathering of risk takers to create Burning Man. This extraordinary freedom would act as a catalyst for new and exciting work simultaneously existing between two worlds: the surrealist photography of early twentieth-century Europe and the Bacchanalian spirit of this world-renowned desert event. Besides, the heroic and fantastic allure of the desert would come to be a key motif in the artist's work, including astonishing aerial photographs.

A Fullness of Form and Emptiness

Will's signature in-motion style gives the impression of a dancing world of loveliness, both in his erotic dancer studies or in the flower series. From Will's erotic portraits to his images of underwater ecologies or the majestic beauty of the desert, one experiences a fullness of form and an emptiness, allowing both balance and intrigue. Will is a creative tour de force whose luxuriously beautiful photos intersect with a sense of the analytical; critics say this is a man who makes his subject dance through light, color, and stop-motion photography. There is certain freedom within his waltz with life's images, where bold color, dramatic landscapes, or charged portraits of sexuality merge with quiet spaces.

A Man Fulfilled

Will Roger lives in Gerlach, Nevada, with his partner and muse, Crimson Rose. He remains a steward of the Black Rock Desert region, where he continues to lend a hand to projects that support the preservation of the land.

Will's life continues to evolve as his magical dance with the Earth revolves to a never-ending tune of the three centers of his life. This dance is not over; it is just the beginning.

Additional Resources

Manifesto for a Burning Age

We are all asleep: REALIZE the Paradigm Shift.

I would like to propose an idea that I have been thinking about for a few years now. We are all asleep, trained from birth to be members of a civilization bent on destroying our human habitat. This civilization thrives by taking resources from the Earth to create a bloated lifestyle that ignores the delicate balance needed to maintain our lives on this planet Earth. Let us look at what needs to be changed in the dominant culture to restore balance toward healing the Earth, humanity, and all living creatures.

During the Bronze Age, as we departed from the 2,000,000-years of how Homo erectus had lived on this planet in harmony and began to mine the Earth's resources and develop agriculture, our population began to increase. During the Industrial Revolution, we began to use coal and oil to mechanize and manufacture. Men and women's roles changed to support an increasing population that industry needed to create more profit. We created religions that supported the dominant culture and underscored our dominance over the Earth. We developed belief systems and languages that supported this dominance. Chauvinism, competition, greed, profit, wealth accumulation, consumerism, superiority, and individualism became the operative constructs that our dominant culture required. It is in our language, education, politics, entertainment, economics, and who we think we are!

Yes, our thoughts, which is our dominant culture's language, help define our role in its support.

It is time to wake up and become the who that we are. One Earth. One Humanity. We are all human. The Earth is a rock tumbling through the universe. It had water and the correct elements and conditions to create simple life forms. Throughout billions of years, the Earth created all the flora and fauna that exist or ever existed, including humans. Everything we perceive on Earth was created by the Earth or its resources. Creation energy is Earth energy, and they are inseparable.

We need to start worshiping the Earth again and recognize her as our Mother.

We are all asleep, drugged by the life we live to support the dominant culture (some call it the economy or capitalism).

The present pandemic has caused a small crack in the illusion that we are forced to live. Maybe it is a wakeup call from the Earth Mother. The men in power want the economy to return to normal because that is where their profit is. We live in a culture whose foundation is flawed. Instead of caring, nurturing in harmony with all life on Earth and with each other, we live a life of greed, competition, dominance, and arrogance to believe that we and our way of life are superior. All the while, this very culture and economy are destroying our habitat for the continuation of human life on this planet. Our way of life in this dominant culture is a learned behavior—we are not born with it. We learn our roles, behaviors, likes and dislikes, allegiances, political systems, and belief systems. All of it is learned from the brainwashing we get from living in this culture. We think we have freedom. What we have is just an illusion of it. Right now, we have the opportunity to reboot, change the way we live on this planet, and become the who that we are. While most will see this paradigm shift as impractical, delusional, I say that the reaction is based on our conditioning from the dominant culture for its preservation.

Here's what we need to do as I see it.

Deconstruction

1. Stop all mining and oil production.

2. Stop big agriculture.

3. Stop all new plastic production.

4. Ban and dismantle all corporations except for non-profits.

5. Drop all national boundaries.

6. Honor, revere, worship the Earth above all other deities.

7. Eliminate prejudices, barriers, obstacles, and boundaries toward gender, race, beliefs, and locations.

8. Eliminate special interest lobbying from all governments. Eliminate government wherever possible.

9. Eliminate the War Machine (military, industrial, corporate complex).

10. Eliminate money.

Construction

1. Plant trees.

2. Establish One Earth, One Humanity.

3. Retool all manufacturing to use only renewable and sustainable resources.

4. Everyone has a garden.

5. Economy based on equality, local distribution, and gifting.

6. Free essential medical/medicine for everyone.

7. Education system where art and science are equal.

8. Women are revered as more than equal as the bearers of life. Women have full sovereignty.

9. Create a system where nurturing and healing are revered above all else.

10. Recreate an educational system that supports all of the above.

The Earth Mother will do what she needs to do to wake up humanity or eliminate humanity. We make the change with intention, or we resist, clutching to a diseased culture. Either way, the time of change, the time of waking up, is here!

A good place to start waking up is to become the observer of your thoughts; become aware. See your place on this planet, see the miracle of life. Seek out the awe, become mindful of the magic that is all around you. Then, begin to believe in the magic again.

The very core of our dominant culture is flawed. Begin to worship the Earth, the home of all life. Understand that we humans are intertwined with all life on this planet, our Earth Mother. What makes humans the same is much greater than what makes us different. See this and love all humans as brothers and sisters.

Do not be afraid to be radical in your thoughts and actions. Be fearless. The future of our life on this planet depends on it!

Wake up to the miracle of life on this planet. Become a caretaker, a nurturer, a healer. There's magic in this as you become more engaged with the power of the Earth. Wake up to the predicament that we are all in. And above all, be fearless in making the changes that are needed right now.

We can build a new culture, a new way of life that is harmonious, sustainable, renewable, and regenerative if we only make an effort to wake up!

Ten Principles of Burning Man

Larry Harvey

Radical Inclusion

Anyone may be a part of Burning Man. We welcome and respect the stranger, and no prerequisites exist for participation in our community.

Gifting

Burning Man is devoted to acts of gift-giving. The value of a gift is unconditional. Gifting does not contemplate a return or an exchange for something of equal value.

Decommodification

In order to preserve the spirit of gifting, our community seeks to create social environments that are unmediated by commercial sponsorships, transactions, or advertising. We stand ready to protect our culture from such exploitation. We resist the substitution of consumption for participatory experience.

Radical Self-Reliance

Burning Man encourages the individual to discover, exercise, and rely on their inner resources.

Radical Self-Expression

Radical self-expression arises from the unique gifts of the individual. No one other than the individual or a collaborating group can determine its content. It is offered as a gift to others. In this spirit, the giver should respect the rights and liberties of the recipient.

Communal Effort

Our community values creative cooperation and collaboration. Therefore, we strive to produce, promote and protect social networks, public spaces, works of art, and methods of communication that support such interaction.

Civic Responsibility

We value civil society. Community members who organize events should assume responsibility for public welfare and communicate civic responsibilities to participants. They must also assume responsibility for conducting events in accordance with local, state, and federal laws.

Leaving No Trace

Our community respects the environment. We are committed to leaving no physical trace of our activities wherever we gather. We clean up after ourselves and endeavor, whenever possible, to leave such places in a better state than when we found them.

Participation

Our community is committed to a radically participatory ethic. Whether in the individual or society, we believe that transformative change can occur only through the medium of deeply personal participation. We achieve being through doing. Everyone is invited to work, and everyone is invited to play. We make the world real through actions that open the heart.

Immediacy

Immediate experience is, in many ways, the most important touchstone of value in our culture. We seek to overcome barriers that stand between us and recognizing our inner selves, the reality of those around us, participating in society, and connecting with a natural world exceeding human powers. No idea can be a substitute for this experience.

Practices: How Do We Get There From Here

- **Intention**
  - Everything we do can be done with the right intention.
  - Bring the art spirit, creation energy, to all your actions.
  - The right intentions are love, creation, healing, nurturing, acceptance, and forgiveness.

- **Cultivating the Three Centers to make the Fourth (Spirit)**
  - Activate the intellectual, emotional, and physical centers each day.
    - Intellectual: critical thinking, problem-solving, intellectual discourse, focused reading.
    - Physical: run/jog, dance, workout, yoga, fast walking, etc.
    - Emotional: laugh, cry, love.
  - Do an activity for each one that does not have the inner voice interfering. Intensity matters.

- **Create a Ritual that involves all Three Centers**
  - Doing daily creates balance to allow the Spirit (Fourth Center) to enter and thrive.
    - Walking (Physical)
    - Engage Feelings (Emotional)
    - Critical Thinking (Intellectual)

The labyrinth works for me as I walk my path (physical), engage my feelings (emotional), and activate my critical thinking (intellectual).

- **The Inner Voice**

  - Become the observer of your inner voice. Let it run and be aware of the dialogue.

    - The Zen sitting meditation is suitable for this.

  - The inner voice is not you; it is what you have come to believe because of how the dominant culture has instilled a pattern of thinking within us to keep the dominant culture in power. Therefore, we must fight off those thoughts.

  - Change the dialogue. Affirmations are a valuable tool for this.

  - Use a different way of communicating; change the language.

  - Bliss and enlightenment happens when your inner voice is silenced, often by awe.

  - Be present with your five senses. Awareness of all five senses at once can still the inner voice.

- **Expectations**

  - Before expecting a change in others, make those changes within yourself first.

  - As you transform yourself inwardly, look to see how you can help others outwardly.

  - If you expect something from another, express it to them. This will ameliorate any disappointment.

- **Activate Your Senses**

  - With intention, become aware of your five senses.

- At first, one at a time and then begin to add them together until all five are running in your awareness.

- When all five senses are running in your awareness, the inner voice naturally stops, and you enter full awareness.

- Sensory experiences are ways of bringing the world inside.

  - Use food for the cultivation of your creative energy.

  - Awaken to a higher state of consciousness.

- **Connecting With Our Ancestors**

  - Learn about your heritage.

  - Discover the myths and legends of your ancestors.

  - This history informs the 'who that you are;

    - A cornerstone belief in indigenous cultures is their respect for the ancestors who gave the people their codes of ethics, religion, spirituality, and morality.

    - This is almost always Earth-centered.

  - Take a course or study the histories of indigenous cultures.

    - Travel, visit. Go to the Hopi Mesas. Go to Lake Titicaca. Go to Myanmar.

  - Understand a totemic relationship to nature.

  - Buy a planisphere and learn the constellations.

- Connect your senses with running water, migrating birds, the primal scream, laughing and drumming, thunder and lightning.

- Any experience that has been repeated since the beginnings of Homo Erectus (roughly 2 million years) can connect to the magic of the Earth, the universe.

- Where did your ancestors walk, and do they now whisper?

- At what point in this cycle are we now?

  - For those of us who did not inherit much or hold any connection to our lineage, how can we rightfully participate within these realms, rituals, and rites of passage?

- **Archetypes**

  - Be open to the world of dreams.

    - Photographer Minor White taught his students, "We know how to photograph something for what it is; learn how to photograph for what else it is." Apply this to yourself. What else are you besides who you think you are? Find your archetype.

  - Be present in your physical body.

    - Contemplate each of your body functions, inside and outward. What do these mean?

    - Think about your mortality.

    - Walk, look, sit, stand still, remain silent while listening.

  - Prayer

- An often-misunderstood practice. It isn't necessarily about seeking salvation, forgiveness, or assistance, though it can be.

- Prayer helps you understand your humble state and that you are only a tiny part of a much larger whole.

- Prayer is a form of affirmation shared with devotion.

- **Ritual**

  - Repetitions of movement, words, thoughts, and contemplations reinforce your growing awareness.

    - Rituals, like prayer, do not necessarily require certain locations. However, when you recognize a place or space as having an identifiable quality of essence, use this place to repeat your rituals. The ritual is thereby identified with and reinforced by the sacredness that already exists.

    - Practice your own rituals but learn of others. The Chinese practice of the *I Ching*.

    - Organize your rituals that follow cycles such as seasons, days, notable personal experiences, honoring certain people... use your imagination and find something personal.

    - Bring others into your circle of rituals. They mean more when practiced with others. Think of Buddhists walking around the Boudha stupa in Kathmandu or religious pilgrims or moments of celebration.

- **Meditate**
    - This is not necessarily a ritual. There are several practices of meditation. Learn and use the one that matches your intention and desired results.
    - Find the magic.
    - Believe in magic. If you don't believe in magic, there is no magic.
    - Learn how to see the magic that knows no location, knows no bounds. It is omnipresent.

- **Practice Art and Learn Techniques of Visualization**
    - Carry a box of colors, a camera, a journal wherever you go. Do this while hiking or walking somewhere, such as to the park or through your neighborhood.
    - Find themes and a narrative you can create and share them on social media, with family, and small on-demand books you can give away as gifts.

- **Random Acts of Kindness and Gift-Giving**
    - Read Lewis Hyde's *The Gift*.
    - Random also means spontaneous.

- **Form Small Communities of Like-Minded People**
    - You can go it alone, but the collective energy shared by a group can be shared, and the growth of others will turbocharge your individual growth.

- **Crack a Book**

- Your education will make you a better speaker, artist, writer, and activist.

  - As part of your education, create your own syllabus, choose your own adventure of learning. Any good syllabus requires a set of practices and sets learning objectives and takeaways.

  - Knowing what you need to know to be an activist will guide your reading and your course of learning.

- **Get Back to the Garden (of Eden)**

  - Honor the Earth by involving yourself with her creation energy.

  - Plant a garden.

  - Plant trees.

  - Create a Community Garden with your friends and neighbors.

    - If you do not have access to a garden space, add potted plants to your living space. Certain varieties of plants are good at cleaning the air and adding oxygen.

  - It's important to have direct contact with the earth.

  - Spend quality time in nature.

    - Daily walks in the park.

    - Camping trips.

    - Honor the sun/moon rise and set.

    - Stargazing.

- **Places of Power**
  - Find/create your personal place of power.
    - Make it unique with your art, totems, burn incense, etc.
    - Ritualize that place.
    - Go there regularly.
  - Spend time at the Earth's great places of power.
    - Places like Machu Pichu, the Great Pyramids, Niagara Falls are recognized for their incredible power that causes awe. There are many such places, and some are near you wherever you are. So, spend some time in awe at these places.

Notes Toward Intellectual Independence

Bertrand Russell

- Do not feel absolutely certain of anything.

- Do not think it is worthwhile to produce belief by concealing evidence, for the evidence is sure to come to light.

- Never try to discourage thinking, for you are sure to succeed.

- When you meet with opposition, even if it should be from your husband or your children, endeavor to overcome it by argument and not by authority, for a victory dependent upon authority is unreal and illusory.

- Have no respect for the authority of others, for there are always contrary authorities to be found.

- Do not use power to suppress opinions you think pernicious, for if you do, the opinions will suppress you.

- Do not fear to be eccentric in opinion, for every opinion now accepted was once eccentric.

- Find more pleasure in intelligent dissent than in passive agreement, for if you value intelligence as you should, the former implies a deeper agreement than the latter.

- Be scrupulously truthful, even when the truth is inconvenient, for it is more inconvenient when you try to conceal it.

- Do not feel envious of the happiness of those who live in a fool's paradise, for only a fool will think that it is happiness.

- It is only necessary to open the doors of our hearts and minds to let the imprisoned demons escape, and the beauty of the world take possession.

In Search of the Mystical Image, Syllabus © 1984

created this syllabus in 1985 and the curriculum was considered to be very progressive for its time. I focused heavily on the works by Robert A. Johnson, a noted lecturer and Jungian analyst.

If I were to teach this class today, I would include a more comprehensive scope of study which would include materials addressing diversity, equity, and inclusivity. I am delighted to see that Johnson has published new editions of his series as recent as 2020.

Weekly Image Projects

I. Read *Way of the Peaceful Warrior* by Dan Millman.

    Review the death-themed work of various artists.

    Illustrate your death.

II. Gender, Same

    If male, read *He: Understanding Masculine Psychology* by Robert A. Johnson.

    If female, read *She: Understanding Feminine Psychology* by Robert A. Johnson.

    Illustrate your same gender.

III. Gender, Opposite

    If male, read *She: Understanding Feminine Psychology* by Robert A. Johnson.

    If female, read *He: Understanding Masculine Psychology* by Robert A. Johnson.

    Illustrate the opposite gender in you.

IV. Man and Woman

Read *We: Understanding the Psychology of Romantic Love* by Robert A. Johnson.

Illustrate communion between a man and a woman.

V. Joy, Ecstasy

Read *Ecstasy: Understanding the Psychology of Joy* by Robert A. Johnson.

Illustrate your supreme ecstasy.

VI. Weakness–Fear

Self-Analysis (Be Honest)

Illustrate your greatest weakness or fear.

VII. Altars–Artifacts

Read *Creative Visualization: Use the Power of Your Imagination to Create What You Want in Your Life* by Shakti Gawain.

Create your altar with your special objects.

Photograph your altar.

The Way of the Common Shaman

Here you see humanity in its most beautiful state with a shared intention and unconditional love. At Burning Man, there is a connection to the Earth that is caring and nurturing. You can't avoid it when you walk around and see humanity in a different light, at least for the time you're there.

The questions arising from what we experience and learn at Burning Man are, can we take that home with us? Can we change the world that way? That's what I'm trying to attempting.

The Inner Voice

When it comes to the inner voice, I wrote as clearly as I could about the ideas that I have, but I also recognize that these are just words on paper. When people read what I write, their inner voice, experience, and cultural context will morph and will then change my ideas into something new.

If it is possible to still our inner voice and if we can be present to the energy that flows around us, I believe it may establish the ground for serendipity. This is the key element in my work. Our inner voice is always there, but it should be our ability not to be affected by it. But, unfortunately, we are.

I look at my life and there were definitely times when my life changed because I could see the influence present there for me. I accepted it. There are probably thousands of other moments where there were powerful influences, but I could not see it or be receptive to it.

I think that some people live their whole lives without ever being able to see the difference. It takes an intention and mindset that is open and clear to be able to do so.

Post-Consumerism

We need to be stronger and more intentional when the dominant culture is forcing us to be consumers. We can be the creative engines that generate vibrant nurturing and healing for others. This is what it means to be a shaman. Yeah, that's the common shaman in each of us. It's there, just not accepted by the denials and ignorance of the dominant culture surrounding us. Instead of always taking and consuming, we need to learn how to shift our behaviors toward being givers and creators.

Gifting

In the act of gifting, you're spreading the joy of what it is to be human. Giving away what we have is also a form of gifting. That creates the pleasure of letting go in some ways, no longer feeling encumbered by possessions. This brings freedom of mind and spirit. There is a creative force in gifting. I think it opens your heart to create a connection between human to human and human to the Earth.

For many people, gifting implies a material object, but it doesn't have to. For example, you could give the gift of song or dance. The best gift to offer anyone is unconditional love without expectation.

Affirmations

Change requires using intentional language. This is called an affirmation. There are many types of affirmations that you can choose from or create for yourself. One affirmation I use every day is, "I am love, energy, and power." Unconditional love is the energy it takes to make an individual change. Then, that love becomes the power it takes to change the world.

When I walk into the labyrinth each evening, before I begin saying the names, I say, "I am in the cosmic flow. I am the cosmic. We are all connected. I am connected."

Walking The Labyrinth and The Sunset Circle

What I do at first is recognize that I'm human, and I walk. I can bring attention to it. And that my intention is connectivity. I intend to connect with all the other humans that have ever walked or are walking now. I am on my way to connect with each of those 73 people I call the Sunset Circle. These are dear friends and family with whom I have developed special relationships over the years. All of them have walked the labyrinth at some point.

At sunset, I become part of the planetary cycle. So, I recognize that I'm like all the other humans that have ever lived. I'm standing and walking, and there's a connection with our earliest human ancestors there. So, watching this sunset is something that we've done since the beginning of our species.

When I go into the labyrinth, I activate my five senses. That's the other thing that all humans have in common: the sensory parts of our beingness. I try to recognize my Three Centers. Walking the labyrinth is my physical center. My emotional center is the unconditional love that I will send to the people in the Sunset Circle and all of humanity. I hear the sound of the spirits of all humankind. I pay attention to that, too. My third center, the intellectual, is when I open my mind to the ideas and thoughts generated through the experience of walking the labyrinth, the shape and concept of that being an intellectual reminder of how our minds work.

While in the labyrinth, my intention is to release my expectations and my desires. When I emerge from that inner path of walking, I have let go of the expectations my inner voice imposes upon me. I'm no different than you or anybody else. But I hope the work I do inside of myself will extend outward to demonstrate the strange and mysterious connections among people, even if separated by time and space. It is easy to say we are all connected. My walk into and out of the labyrinth offers proof that there it is true.

Ritual

Let's bring an intention of connecting to the magic that envelopes the entire Earth. We simultaneously connect with The Great Spirit, or Gaia, or God, whatever you name this numinous quality of the universe. That is the foundation of any form of ritual practice: acknowledge the mystery. When we envision our practices, we do so with clarity and focus. There must be a purpose with an outcome. With that form of creation energy, I think you can determine and create your own rituals.

Being on The Edge

You can choose to follow many different paths in life. You can take the safe way at every step to give you security and predictability. I think it's better to walk on the edge all the time. Finding our edge is uncertain, unlike the path of certainty. It opens the way ahead of unexpected turns, not knowing what hides around the bend. Those are the experiences we cherish as we grow older. Allow for a life of synchronicity. Your edge will also change as you grow older.

I used to be able to climb mountains and backpack and cross the rushing waters of streams. I can barely do any of that anymore. My body doesn't let me, though my mind says, do it. But I still have my edges that challenge my mind and body. I explore the Black Rock Desert that is the landscape where I dwell. It is vast and, at times, uncertain. The uncertainties of our journeys are what opens us to receive the magic and beauty of the universe.

Finding Your Way

You need to find your own way through the world, but with a common goal for all of humanity. We want to change our culture to live a sustainable, harmonious life as one world, one humanity. It doesn't matter how you get there. It doesn't matter what tools you use to affect healthy and meaningful change. There are many tools available to us, and in this book, I point out ones that I've used. But our dilemmas, challenges, and histories are personal to us. So, everyone needs to be led by their history.

Honoring The Human Spirit

Whenever you interact with another human, your intention should be to honor their spirit. I think it's something that we must work at. Arrogantly, we often approach a situation where we interact without acknowledging who that person is on the inside. Our best relationships begin when our spirit meets that of the other person. While we may be conversing on the surface, energies within us are connecting, forging what may become a lasting relationship of mutual respect and love.

One Humanity, One Earth

When I say harmony, I mean a balance with all the other life forms and nonlife forms on the planet. The minerals and rocks possess an internal force of energy with a vibrant spirit, just as everything else in the world. There's no room for error anymore. We need to help everyone see the beauty for humanity is that there is only one Earth.

Change

At Burning Man, you will see the synchronicities that create the connections, the unconditional love, and the gifting of all those magical things. Going there actually changes people's lives. It can change your life.

A desert is a sacred place that is demanding. It compels you to feel in awe of its beauty and harshness.

Index of Photography

Contributors

Rosa JH Berland is a curator specializing in modern art and design. A published author, she has worked for The Museum of Modern Art, The Guggenheim Museum, The Whitney Museum of American Art, and the Frick Collection. She serves as the Chief Curator of The Objects Foundation, New York and as the Director of the Edward Boccia Artist Trust, St. Louis.

Chip Conley is the New York Times bestselling author of *Wisdom@Work: The Making of a Modern Elder.* He founded Modern Elder Academy (MEA), the world's first "midlife wisdom school," where attendees learn how to repurpose a lifetime of experience for the modern workplace. He serves on the board of the Encore.org, and the advisory board for the Stanford Center for Longevity.

Fred Sigman is an art historian, photographer, and author of the award-winning book, *Motel Vegas.* The last twenty years he has written about, photographed and filmed ancient architectural landscapes throughout Mexico, Peru and a dozen countries in Asia. He currently teaches online as a Professor of Art History for the College of Southern Nevada while maintaining his globetrotting lifestyle from his home in Siem Reap, Cambodia.

Lightning Source UK Ltd.
Milton Keynes UK
UKRC030003160223
417096UK00004B/15

9798985100310